LAST MINUTE SPEAKING

A SURVIVAL TOOLKIT

Jana,
Thank you so much for your kind words and support for this book!
Stuart Pink
7/10/23

STUART PINK

"Pink does a brilliant job of laying out a process for developing one's speech from concept to performance. By creating three books in one, he's provided a reasonable method for any speech giver, no matter what phase of development, no matter how seasoned or novice, and no matter what amount of time available. *Last Minute Speaking – A Survival Toolkit*, is a fantastic book."

- **LINDA STACY**, Podcast Host, Work Dope

"This is an amazing resource for a speaker at any level. This book is detailed and expansive, stuffed with tools, tips, and recommendations for the what, why, how, and where of writing and delivering a speech. Most importantly, this book has tips on preparing for a last minute speech, which his tools make much easier to handle. The book is written in a relaxed, easily accessible style. I only wish I had this book in my hands when I took my first steps in public speaking many years ago in Toastmasters. This book is like a big comfortable pillow to release and let go of your fears of public speaking. This book is a worthy investment for any potential speaker or a well-seasoned veteran. Read and read it again - a wonderful book!"

- **JANA SCHOLTEN**, Bestselling author of *Enchanted Wellness ~ How To Go From Hating Disease To Loving It!* and Wellness Expansion Expert

"Relax, you don't have to be anxious about speaking at the last minute. Stuart Pink's book gives you access to a toolkit with seven tools to help you quickly prepare an interesting and memorable talk. The resources include a time planner, presentation priorities model, and message funnel to assist you in developing a presentation that resonates with your audience even if you only have a few minutes to prepare. If you don't have time to read the full book, you can learn or review the tools in either the included 3-minute or 10-minute version. Stuart's advice is easy to follow, and you'll learn something valuable whether you're a beginner or expert speaker. Use the tools in this book before you give your next talk. You and your audience will be happy you did."

- **RICK POLLAK**, Presentation Coach

"I like the ease of this book and the way it is set up to be quick and easy for the last minute speaker! Clever and efficient! The humor throughout the book is subtle but enjoyable to read. Overall, this book is not only easy to read and follow, but also very thorough and informative!"

- **PAM GARRAMONE**, Positive Psychology Speaker, author of *Be, Happier*

"Stuart Pink's *Last Minute Speaking* guide is a must-have reference book for anyone who wants to hone their presentation skills AND be prepared to be able to speak at the last minute! It is well laid out and full of practical tips and timelines. It really is "The Speaker's Toolkit"."

- **SCOTTIE SPURZEM**, English language coach

"Stuart Pink's book *Last Minute Speaking* is a fantastic read! And a deep accessible resource of information both for beginners and experts in the world of public speaking. Written in an easygoing, lighthearted style, sprinkled with easy to understand diagrams, this book is wide ranging, covering every aspect of public speaking - from the why, what, and how of writing, to delivering all different types and kinds of speeches. This book should be the go-to resource for public speaking - making public speaking more accessible and less daunting for the beginner, as well as being a deep well of tips and information for expert speakers who may be considering different formats to perform in (i.e. TED talks, panel discussions, competition debating etc.). This is the kind of book, that once you've read it all, you'll feel confident that you can write and deliver any size speech, in any setting, for any length of time, long or short, and make it memorable, impactful, and make a difference for any size audience. And, this book is so full of resources and valuable insights, you'll want to go back to it ongoingly, making you a better and better speaker each time. A book worth your time and energy to read and digest and reread again and again."

- **DAN JUNKINS**, Bestselling author of *Peacocks, Poison and Leukemia: A Life of Vibrant Health*

ISBN: 978-0-9986824-0-2

www.lastminutespeaking.com

This book is dedicated to my wife Kat –
the speaker who changed my life.

CONTENTS

THE SPEAKER'S TOOLKIT 1

Introduction – Presentation Priorities 49

BASIC PRESENTATION SKILLS

Chapter 1 – Context 53

Chapter 2 – Confidence 60

Chapter 3 – Content 94

OH NO! I HAVE TO SPEAK!

THE SPEAKER'S TOOLKIT

Don't worry. I've got you. You're safe now!

Even if you don't have much time, you'll be OK. This book is actually three books that are designed to be used in different ways:

- **EMERGENCY:** Smash glass and get help in a hurry.
- **REFERENCE:** Look up help for a specific aspect of speaking.
- **COMPREHENSIVE GUIDE:** Everything you need to survive your speech is in this book. If you wish to go further, read the whole book to take your speaking to a masterful level.

This toolkit has seven tools to help you prepare for your speech:

(1) **Time Planner**

Start here. How much time do you have to prepare? This planner shows you how best to use your time available.

(2) **Quick Help Guide**

Do you have a specific speaking problem that you want help with? This tool lists the most common questions and problems speakers have and where to find answers in this book.

(3) **Top 10 Tips**

Do you want quick results? Here is more than a decade of speaking experience condensed into ten top tips.

(4) **Benefits of Speaking**

Right now, speaking may feel to you like a curse, not a blessing. These benefits of speaking will help change your mindset from having an unwanted obligation to an amazing opportunity.

1

(5) **Last Minute Speaking**: the **3-minute** version of the book
Don't have time to read the full book? Read this in three minutes.

(6) **Last Minute Speaking**: the **10-minute** version of the book
Don't have time to read the full book? Read this in ten minutes.

(7) **Last Minute Speaking**: the **complete book**
And at last, here's the book itself. The book also includes the following additional tools:

- **Presentation Priorities Model** – a complete overview of speaking and what to do first
- **Speech Context Questions** – what you need to ask to be ready to speak
- **The Speaker Nerves Spectrum** – how to manage your nerves
- **The Secret to Confident Speaking** – three key qualities to being confident
- **What's Your Speaker Type?** – four types of speakers (three good, one bad)
- **The Topic Sweet Spot** – how to select your topic
- **The Message Funnel** – how to develop your message
- **Value Filter** – how to ensure your message is valuable
- **Interest Filter** – how to ensure your message is interesting
- **Speech Maps** – how to plan and structure your speech
- **8 Types of Practice** – choose the practice type that suits you the best
- **Modular Practice** – how to vary your speech practice for maximum benefit
- **Basic Public Speaking Skills** – everything you need to know for good speech delivery
- **Checklist for Before Speaking**
- **Checklist for After Speaking**
- **Speech Return on Investment** – how to get maximum results for the effort you put into improving your speech

TIME PLANNER

5 minutes to prepare
- Focus on what your message (main point) is.
- Do you have a story that can go with it?
- Mentally prepare what you are going to say.

30 minutes to prepare

As above +
- Read Top 10 Tips
- Read 3-minute book
- Create a simple Speech Map and structure (e.g., opening – three points – closing).
- Create bullet point notes if helpful.

1 hour to prepare

As above +
- Read Quick Help Guide
- Use the Quick Help Guide to find help with particular issues and skim the relevant chapter to find the solution.

4 hours to prepare

Divide your time up as follows:
- Read Top 10 Tips
- Read 10-minute book
- Read Quick Help Guide
- Gather any materials or information you need.
- Prepare your talk with a simple Speech Map and structure.
- Make any simple notes you need to help you.
- Keep any slides you need to create very simple.
- Leave time to practice. Use the Speech Map to focus on the route of your speech rather than trying to remember specific words.

1 day to prepare

As above +

- Use the extra time to find the best stories and examples to use.
- Don't create your speech up until the last minute. Allow at least one hour to practice and internalize your speech.

3 days to prepare

Similar to above. Ideally, you should have your speech created by the end of the second day so that you can focus on practicing and internalizing on the third day.

1 week to prepare

Similar to above. Try to make as much progress early on as possible and leave a couple of days at the end to practice and internalize.

- Read Top 10 Tips
- Read Quick Help Guide
- Read Benefits of Speaking
- Read The whole book

1 week – 1 month to prepare

As above +

You have enough time to go through more than one draft of your speech, get feedback (if necessary) and improve it. Try to finalize the speech before the last week so you can practice and internalize it then. You also have time to work on speech delivery skills.

Longer than 1 month to prepare

As above +

The sooner you can start collecting ideas, stories, examples, and information, the easier it will be to start outlining your Speech Map. You then have plenty of time to refine and improve it.

Note: The nature of some work presentations may be that certain information necessary for the presentation is only available at the last minute. Try to anticipate this so that such information can be slotted into the presentation whenever it becomes available. This should not affect the overall practice and internalization of your speech. If the structure or the message of your speech keeps changing, it is very hard to properly internalize.

QUICK HELP GUIDE

Below are some of the most common issues and fears that people have when they have to give a speech. If any of these is an issue, you can jump ahead now to the relevant section in the book to put your mind at ease.

Problems answered in Time Planner (previous pages):
- I don't have much time.

Problems answered in Introduction – Presentation Priorities:
- I've got to give a speech and I don't know where to start (also see below).

Problems answered in Chapter 1 – Context:
- I've got to give a speech and I don't know where to start (also see above).
- I don't know what is expected of me.

Problems answered in Chapter 2 – Confidence:
- I'm terrified of speaking.
- I'm afraid of looking stupid or making a mistake.
- I'm afraid of forgetting my speech (also see below).
- I'm afraid of being judged by others.
- I want to calm myself down before speaking.
- I'm tired of my speech and want to get excited about it again.

Problems answered in Chapter 3 – Content:
- I don't know what to say.
- I'm afraid of forgetting my speech (also see above and below).
- I don't know whether to read my speech or use notes.
- I have to prepare slides.
- I want to make my message clear.

Problems answered in Chapter 4 – Communication:

- I hate practicing.
- I don't know how to practice.
- I'm afraid of something happening that I'm not prepared for.
- I'm afraid of forgetting my speech (also see above).
- I'm afraid of my speech being too long or short.
- I'm afraid of the technology going wrong.
- I want to improve my speech delivery skills.

Problems answered in Chapter 5 – Connection:

- I want to make my speech even better.
- I want my speech to be more interesting and engaging.
- I want the audience to love my speech.
- I want to know how to tell stories in speaking.
- I want to be funny when speaking.
- I want my audience to take action.

Problems answered in Chapter 6 – Online Speaking:

- I have to speak online.
- I want to know how to present differently when online.
- I have to decide between in-person, online, or hybrid presenting.

Problems answered in Chapter 7 – Specific Events:

- I have to do one of the following types of speech: work presentation, introduction, thank-you speech, wedding, funeral, acceptance speech, impromptu speaking, job interview, local meeting, panel discussion, pitch, kids' or school presentation, competition debating, Toastmasters contest or TED Talk.

TOP 10 SPEAKING TIPS

1. **Make sure your audience can hear you clearly**.

2. **Focus on your audience**.
   It's not about you. (Don't worry about anything going wrong.)
   It's about them. (Focus on what your audience needs and how they will benefit.)

3. **Use a Speech Map** to plan and deliver your speech. Your Speech Map answers two questions:
   (1) Where am I going? (Your message).
   (2) How do I get there? (Your main points).

4. **Keep it simple**. Use a simple speech structure (e.g., three key points, problem + solution). Use simple (conversational) words and sentences.

5. **Don't memorize the speech.** Internalize the message and route (your main points) and deliver it in your own words.

6. **Tell personal stories** to illustrate points and connect the audience to you.

7. **Stay relevant**. Only use speech content (stories, ideas, etc.) and tools (slides, props, etc.) that are relevant to your speech message.

8. **Don't leave unanswered questions** in the audience's mind. (These are obvious questions they will have about something you said.)

9. **Vary your delivery**. Don't be the same.

10. **Have fun**!

BENEFITS OF SPEAKING

The speaking skills outlined in this book are the skills that you already use every day to speak to people. But using these skills to speak publicly is an opportunity to supercharge the following benefits.

Personal Benefits
- Clarify your thinking.
- Improve your confidence and learn how to control your nerves.
- Get satisfaction by using your skill to help others.
- Develop your creativity and spontaneity.

Work and Career Benefits
- Develop excellent communication skills (both on and off the stage).
- Presenting to others is a path to leadership and career opportunities.
- Speaking to groups is a way to network and multiply your impact.
- Use persuasive skills to make sales, advocate for change and inspire people.
- Public speaking is a future-proof skill. It cannot be computerized or automated.
- Communication, leadership, and advocacy skills make you more valuable and stand out.

Social Benefits
- Improve your relationships with people (by communicating clearly, telling stories, networking, and speaking on special occasions).

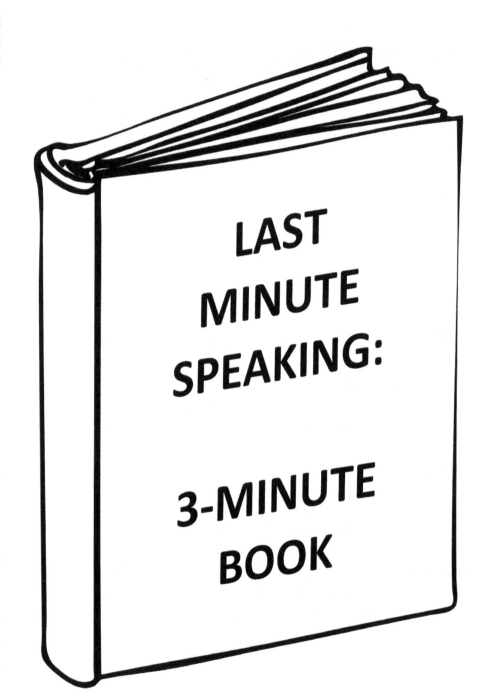

LAST
MINUTE
SPEAKING:

3-MINUTE
BOOK

Presentation Priorities Model

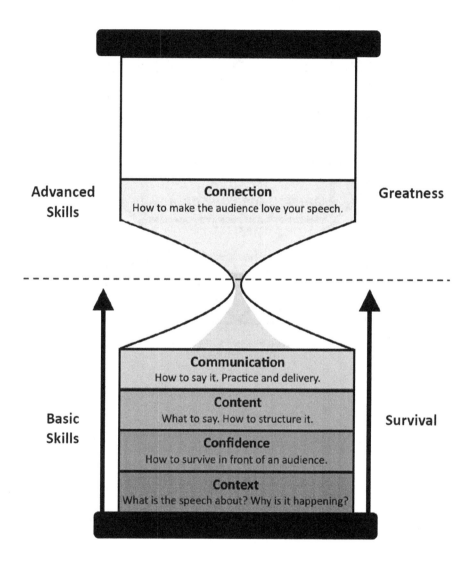

CHAPTER 1 - CONTEXT

Speech Context Questions

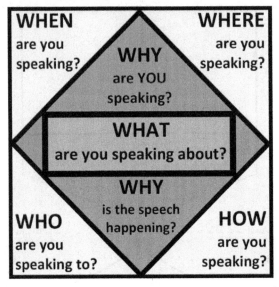

CHAPTER 2 - CONFIDENCE

2.2 Mental Confidence

The Secret to Confident Speaking

FAKE IT till you make it

SERVICE to your AUDIENCE

The power of AUTHENTICITY

Service to Your Audience

Focus on your audience and their needs. What do they want? How will they benefit from your talk?

- **It's not about you - it's about them.** Everyone has their own problems. They're not worrying about you. Help them change their lives for the better.
- **Be passionate about what you are speaking about.**
- **Think of speaking as an opportunity, not an obligation.** Think "today I **GET** to speak" rather than "today I **HAVE** to speak."
- **The audience wants you to succeed.**

- **The audience needs to hear your message.** Otherwise, you are depriving them of something to help them.
- **Think of the audience as individuals.** Focus on the individuals who need your message. Find the friendly faces in the room.

Fake It Till You Make It

- **Visualize success.** Visualize yourself speaking successfully and finishing.
- **Eliminate negative thoughts.**
- **Take control when speaking.** Adjusting your speech, answering questions, and choosing breaks, subtly reinforces that you're in control.

The Power of Authenticity

- **Authentic moments make the best connection and are more memorable.**
- **What's the worst that can happen?** Regardless of how your speech goes, life will still go on and you will be OK.
- **What if things go wrong?** Anticipate as much as possible and keep perspective.
- **What if I blank out and forget everything?** Don't panic. Keep breathing. Continue if you can. If your mind goes completely blank, use your Speech Map (with the overall message and key points) to get back on course.
- **Don't be afraid if you don't know the answer.** No one knows everything.
- **Have fun.** Speaking is much easier when you are having fun.

2.3 Physical Confidence

Your Body's Basics
Focus on adequate sleep, breathing, food, drink, and clothing.

CHAPTER 3 - CONTENT

3.2 Speech Topic – What Are You Speaking About?

Message Ideas

A message helps organize your speech and give it purpose.

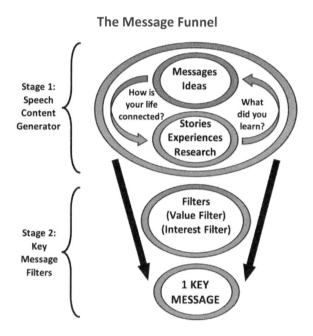

The Message Funnel

The Value Filter

$$Value \quad = \quad \frac{Importance \ x \ Relevance}{Ability \ to \ Implement}$$

The value of a speech to an audience is increased by how important and relevant to them it is. The value is decreased by how difficult the advice is to implement.

The Interest Filter

The less original your message is, the more original your stories, experiences, and delivery must be.

3.3 Speech Maps – How Do You Structure Your Speech?

A speech is a series of ideas with an overall message.
The message is your destination.
The ideas are your journey.

You must answer two key questions:

    (1) WHERE AM I GOING?
    (2) HOW DO I GET THERE?

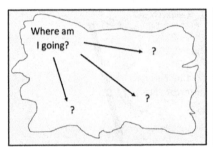 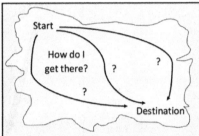

A Speech Map is a visual representation of your speech that shows your overall message (your destination) and ideas on the way (your journey).

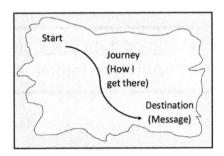

What Does a Speech Map Look Like?

A Speech Map is any form of notes or diagrams that are helpful to you.

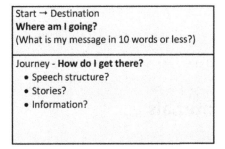

Start → Destination
Where am I going?
(What is my message in 10 words or less?)

Journey - **How do I get there?**
• Speech structure?
• Stories?
• Information?

Creating a Speech Map

Blank Page   Speech Map

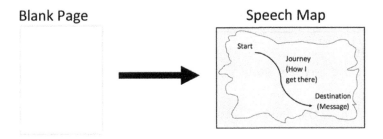

You already know your message. Now choose a simple structure for your speech:

• 3 Key Points
• Chronological
• Problem + Solution

Full Speech   Speech Map

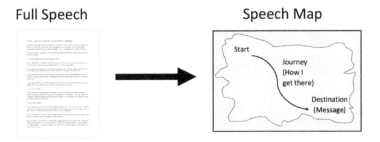

Separate your speech into sections. Label each section. You now have your Speech Map. Decide how detailed you want it to be.

The Introduction

Catch the audience's attention.

Give them a reason to keep listening.

The Closing

Your message should be clear and understood by the audience.

3.4 Speech Materials

Slide Presentations

Only use slides if they help your presentation.

Effective Slide Presentations

Content
   • Use very few words per slide.
   • Use pictures.
   • Make the slides easy to read.

Use and Delivery
   • Explain them in your own words.
   • Reveal one point at a time.
   • Turn slides off when not using them.
   • Practice using slides.
   • Make sure you can give your speech without slides.

CHAPTER 4 – COMMUNICATION

4.1 Speech Style – How Are You Saying It?
A true expert can explain complicated ideas and make them sound so simple that everyone can understand them.

4.2 Practice

Categories of Practice
- **Mental practice.** Practice the whole speech or just the outline anywhere.
- **Read out loud.** Read and pause as you would deliver it.
- **Notes and bullet points speech.** Make sure your notes work for you. Use important words or topic headings or words that will trigger your memory. Will you be able to read your notes?
- **Modular practice.** Break your speech into sections (each new point or story). Practice any section.
- **Timing practice.** Build flexibility into your speech. Calculate what time you should be at each point in your speech.
- **Technology practice.** Have a contingency for technology failing.

The Basic Public Speaking Skills

Voice
- **Clear voice**
- **Volume** - Speak slightly louder than your normal, comfortable voice.
- **Pace** - Don't speak too quickly.

Body Language
- **Eye contact** - Eye contact builds trust.
- **Facial expression** - Be smiling and friendly.
- **Hands** - Hands by your side is most natural.

4.3 Delivery

How is Delivery Different From Practice?
- Whatever you do, the show must go on.
- Personalize a speech by interacting with your audience.
- Manage your time. Keep your speech flexible.

Questions (Q&A)
What if I don't know the answer?
Give the best answer you can and explain what you don't know.

CHAPTER 5 - CONNECTION

5.1 Stories

- **Why stories?** Everyone loves stories. Relive a personal story.
- **The basics:**
  - Who is in it? (Characters)
  - Where and when does it take place? (Setting)
  - What happens? (Plot)
- **Dialogue.** Dialogue brings stories to life.
- **Characters.** Help the audience understand your characters by describing them and their motivations.
- **Don't be the hero of your own story.** Perhaps the hero is the person that helped you achieve your goal.
- **Tension.** A story without tension or conflict is boring. Don't breeze over the moment toward an easy resolution. Can you heighten the tension?
- **Resolve questions.** Don't leave audience members with unresolved questions because this will distract and frustrate them.

5.3 Message Focus

- **What do you want the audience to remember?**
- **How can you get the audience to remember?** Limit points, facts, and statistics. Emphasize, repeat and display key points. Make key points memorable.
- **What do you want the audience to do?** Tell the audience what to do next and make it easy.
- **Translate facts and statistics.** Present facts and statistics in a way that means something to the audience.

LAST
MINUTE
SPEAKING:

10-MINUTE
BOOK

Presentation Priorities Model

Every speaker starts at the bottom. To progress to a higher level, you need to have passed through the lower levels.

Presentation Priorities Model

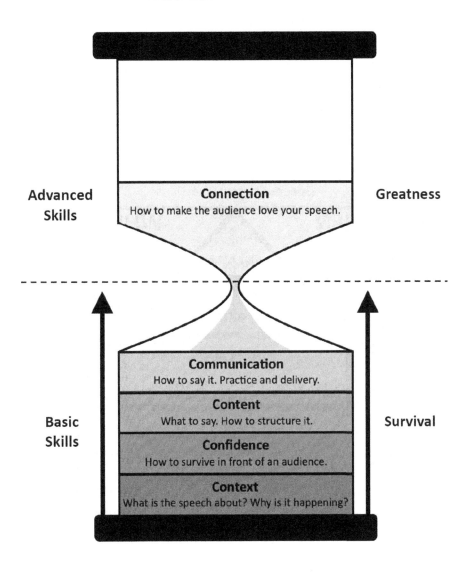

Advanced Skills — Connection — How to make the audience love your speech. — Greatness

Communication — How to say it. Practice and delivery.
Content — What to say. How to structure it.
Confidence — How to survive in front of an audience.
Context — What is the speech about? Why is it happening?

Basic Skills — Survival

CHAPTER 1 - CONTEXT

Speech Requirements
- **What** are you speaking about?
- **Why** are **you** speaking?
- **Why** is the speech happening?

Speech Logistics
- **When** are you speaking?
- **Where** are you speaking?
- **Who** are you speaking to?
- **How** are you speaking?

Speech Context Questions

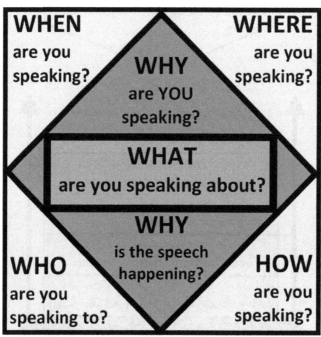

CHAPTER 2 - CONFIDENCE

2.1 Fear

If you fear speaking, control it through confidence.

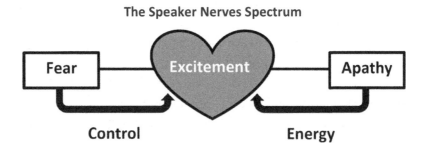

The Speaker Nerves Spectrum

2.2 Mental Confidence

The Secret to Confident Speaking

The core element is service to your audience. Faking it and authenticity appear to be opposites, but work together to complete your confidence.

Service to Your Audience

Focus on your audience and their needs. What do they want? How will they benefit from your talk?

It's not about you - it's about them.
Everyone has their own problems. They're not worrying about you. Help them change their lives for the better.

Be passionate about what you are speaking about
If you don't love your speech, neither will your audience.

Think of speaking as an opportunity, not an obligation
Think "today I **GET** to speak" rather than "today I **HAVE** to speak." What's the opportunity?
- To share an important message?
- To change or improve people's lives?
- Personal growth?

The audience wants you to succeed

The audience needs to hear your message
Otherwise, you are depriving them of something to help them.

Think of the audience as individuals
Focus on the individuals who need your message. Find the friendly faces in the room.

Your audience needs you to be a leader
Someone has to present this important information so why not you?

Fake It Till You Make It

Visualize success
Visualize yourself:

- speaking successfully.
- traveling to the venue.
- giving the speech.
- being on stage.
- looking at the audience.
- answering questions.
- feeling great at the end of your successful speech.

Eliminate negative thoughts

Show the audience you're in control
Be calm and in control, regardless of what you're feeling inside.

Take control when speaking
Little decisions such as adjusting your speech, answering questions, and choosing breaks, subtly reinforce that you're in control.

The Power of Authenticity

Authentic moments make the best connection
Authenticity shows you are in the moment.

Authentic moments are more memorable
Authentic moments (such as mistakes) can be funny and help your presentation come alive.

What's the worst that can happen?
There is no physical threat in speaking. Regardless of how your speech goes, life will still go on and you will be OK.

What if things go wrong?
Anticipate as much as possible that could go wrong. Keep perspective over unforeseen problems. Be a calm, professional leader.

What if I blank out and forget everything?
Don't panic. Keep breathing. Continue if you can. Add in what you forgot later when you remember. The audience will never know. If your mind goes completely blank, use your Speech Map (with the overall message and key points) to get back on course.

Be imperfect but not incompetent
Everyone makes mistakes, but be competent.

Failures are learning opportunities

The value of humor
If something unexpected and funny happens, just accept it and laugh.

Don't be afraid if you don't know the answer
No one knows everything. It is fine to say you don't know the answer.

Have fun
Speaking is much easier when you are having fun.

How do you choose between faking it and authenticity?
Ask yourself, **"What will make the audience's experience better?"** The audience's experience will be improved by anything which makes them:
- better understand your material.
- connect with you.
- laugh.

2.3 Physical Confidence

Your Body's Basics
- **Sleep**: Be well rested.
- **Breathing**: Slow, deep breathing can help calm you.
- **Food**: Eat far enough in advance that it will not interfere with your energy levels.

- **Drink**: Water is best. Avoid needing a bathroom break while speaking.
- **Clothing**: Wear clothing and shoes that are appropriate but also comfortable. Practice speaking in this clothing.

Routine
If it helps, develop a routine before speaking such as focusing on the basics above, walking, listening to music, or looking at your Speech Map.

Your presentation begins when you can be seen
Project confidence at all times to maximize your audience's comfort.

Body Language
Stand up straight, look people in the eyes and move purposefully on stage.

Voice
Your voice can project confidence that you might not be feeling inside.

2.4 Energy

From Apathy to Excitement
Generate energy to make you more excited by:
- changing your speech.
- making your speech more interactive (through questions, exercises, or humor).
- finding things to look forward to.
- thinking about how important your message is.
- increasing your physical energy before speaking.

CHAPTER 3 - CONTENT

3.1 Speech Purpose – Why Are You Speaking?

Speeches are better if they have all three purposes in them as each speech purpose complements the others.

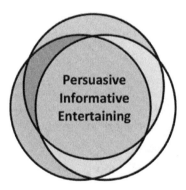

3.2 Speech Topic – What Are You Speaking About?

Topic Ideas

First, follow any specific requirements you have been given. Then consider:

1. What are you passionate about?
2. What does the audience want?

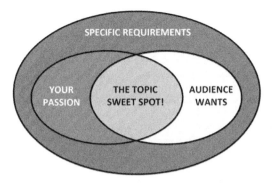

Message Ideas

A message in a speech:

- gives your speech purpose and meaning.
- helps organize and give it direction.
- gives the audience a clear, valuable benefit from listening to you.

The Message Funnel

The Message Funnel has two stages to help you create content and refine it down to a key message.

The Message Funnel

Stage 1:
Speech
Content
Generator

Messages Ideas

How is your life connected?

What did you learn?

Stories
Experiences
Research

Stage 2:
Key
Message
Filters

Filters
(Value Filter)
(Interest Filter)

1 KEY
MESSAGE

Stage 1: Speech Content Generator

Start at any point and continue around until you have enough content.

1. Think about possible ideas and messages.
2. Ask how your life or work is connected to these.
3. This should lead to stories, experiences, or research.
4. Ask what you learned from these stories, experiences, or research.

Stage 2: Key Message Filters

Most speeches benefit from having one key message. Avoid a long list of unconnected ideas, messages, or stories.

The Value Filter

The best service you can give your audience is value.

$$\text{Value} \quad = \quad \frac{\text{Importance x Relevance}}{\text{Ability to Implement}}$$

The value of a speech to an audience is increased by how important and relevant to them it is. The value is decreased by how difficult the advice is to implement.

The Interest Filter

To keep the audience interested, the less original your message is, the more original your stories, experiences, and delivery must be.

The Interest Filter

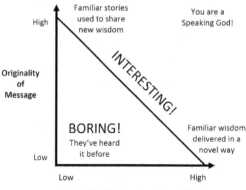

Originality of Stories, Experiences & Delivery

3.3 Speech Maps – How Do You Structure Your Speech?

The biggest mistake speakers make is to focus more on writing than thinking about what they are actually going to say. A speech should be more like a conversation.

What is a speech?

A speech is a series of ideas with an overall message.
The message is your destination.
The ideas are your journey.

You must answer two key questions:
    (1) WHERE AM I GOING?
    (2) HOW DO I GET THERE?

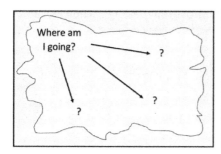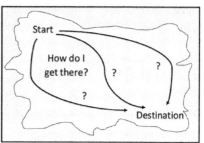

A Speech Map is a visual representation of your speech that shows your overall message (your destination) and ideas on the way (your journey).

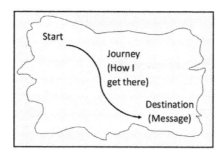

A Speech Map makes it easier for you to remember your speech and easier for your audience to understand it.

What does a Speech Map look like?

A Speech Map is any form of notes or diagrams that are helpful to you.

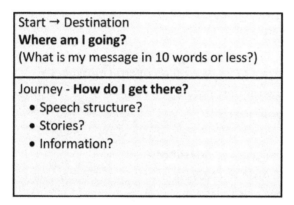

Start → Destination
Where am I going?
(What is my message in 10 words or less?)

Journey - **How do I get there?**
- Speech structure?
- Stories?
- Information?

Where am I going? - Thinking about your overall message. The clearer it is, the better it is.

How do I get there? - Choose the route that makes the most sense and that the audience will understand and appreciate best. **Everything you include should help explain your message and get you to your destination.**

Creating a Speech Map

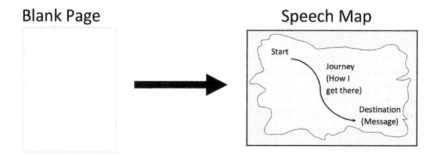

Blank Page   Speech Map

Speech Structures

You already know your message. Now choose a simple structure for your speech:

- **3 Key Points**
- **Chronological**
- **Problem + Solution**
- **Spatial** (the relationship between people or places)
- **Demonstration:** (1) What is it? (2) Why is it needed? (3) What problem does it solve?

Full Speech   Speech Map

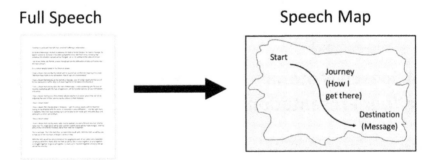

Draw lines across your speech separating each new section (any new point or story). Label each section so you can see the journey from start to destination. You now have your Speech Map. Decide how detailed you want it to be. If you are worried about forgetting something important, put it on the Speech Map.

The Introduction

Catch the audience's attention:

1. Story
2. Startling Statement
3. Question
4. Interesting Statistic/Fact
5. Humor (not joke)
6. Captivating Quotation

Give them a reason to keep listening

- **Curiosity** – Tease the audience with something they want to find out.
- **Value** – Be a gold mine of valuable information from the outset.
- **Entertainment** and **surprise** – Get the audience to enjoy your presentation from the start.

The Closing

Your message should be clear and understood by the audience. Some tips to close well:

- Link back to the beginning
- Don't rush
- Finish on time
- Call to action

3.4 Speech Materials – What Else Do You Need for Your Presentation?

Slides

Only use slides if they help your presentation.

Effective Slide Presentations - Content
Do: - Use very few words per slide. - Use pictures, video, or media that you couldn't otherwise show. - Make the slides clear and easy to read. - Carefully proof and edit your slides. **Don't:** - Make text heavy slides. - Use copyrighted images. - Have too many slides. - Make slides too distracting.

Effective Slide Presentations - Use and Delivery

Do:

- Explain them in your own words.
- Reveal one point at a time.
- Turn slides off when not using them.
- Make sure you practice using them.
- Make sure you can give your speech without slides.

Don't:

- Read through them, adding nothing else.
- Reveal a long list of points.
- Stand in front of the projector.
- Use slides for the first time when giving your presentation.

CHAPTER 4 – COMMUNICATION

4.1 Speech Style – How Are You Saying It?

You are speaking to share your message and ideas. A true expert can explain complicated ideas and make them sound so simple that everyone can understand them.

4.2 Practice

Categories of Practice

Practice is the rehearsal of any part of your speech to make it better.

Mental Practice

Mental practice is great because you can do it anywhere, at any time, and practice the whole speech or just the outline.

Read Out Loud
Fully-Written Speech
- Read at the pace you would deliver it.
- Pause in appropriate places.
- Emphasize the same words you would when speaking on stage.

Notes and Bullet Points Speech

Make sure that your notes work for you.

- Do you have the correct words written down? (Most important words or topic headings or words that will trigger your memory.)
- Do you have the fewest words possible written down?
- Will you be able to read your notes?

Modular Practice

Break your speech into sections. Each section represents a new point or story in your speech. Practice any section of your speech and focus on how to transition from one section to the next.

Floor Modular Practice (Stage Mapping)

To practice stage movement through modular practice, put a numbered sheet of paper on the floor for each section with one or two keywords on. Then give the speech standing at each sheet of paper and practice moving between the different sections.

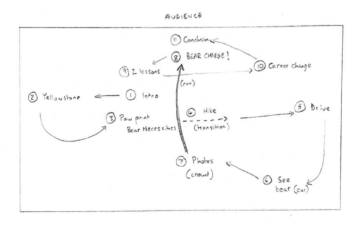

Timing Practice

- It is always better to finish early rather than late.
- Build flexibility into your speech.

- Know how long each section is and how important all the different sections are, so you can skip the least important part of your speech if you need to save time.
- Each of the main points or sections in your speech is a waypoint. Calculate in advance at what time you should be at each waypoint in your speech.

Technology Practice
Have a contingency plan for technology failing.

Slides are not the presenter!
- Don't just read the slide.
- Don't hide behind the slides.
- Don't use the slides as a crutch. Using slides as a prompt is OK if you add value to them.
- Don't stand in front of the slide.

Public Speaking Skills Practice
Focus on one skill at a time.

The Basic Public Speaking Skills

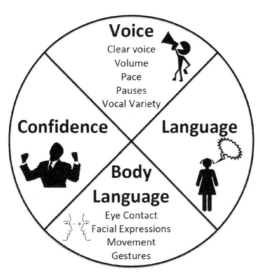

Voice

Using your voice is the most important basic skill.

- **Clear voice.** Pronounce your words as clearly as possible.
- **Volume.** Speak slightly louder than your normal, comfortable voice.
- **Pace.** Don't speak too quickly.
- **Pauses.** Pauses are very important. They emphasize points, give the audience time to reflect, and add drama and tension.
- **Vocal variety.** Variety and contrast are important to keep the audience's attention.

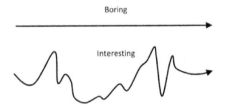

- **Warming up.** Humming is a gentle exercise for the throat that you can do very quietly.

Language

Slow down and control the words that come out of your mouth.

Body Language

- **Eye contact.** Eye contact with your audience builds trust and credibility and allows you to monitor your audience.
- **Facial expression.** Be smiling and friendly.
- **Hands.** Putting your hands by your side is the most natural thing to do.
- **Feet.** If you have a choice, come out from behind a lectern because it can act as a barrier between you and your audience.

4.3 Delivery

How is Delivery Different From Practice?

- **You only get one chance**. Whatever you do, the show must go on.
- **Energy.** Your energy levels are likely to be significantly higher.
- **Breathing.** Remember to keep breathing properly and use breathing to calm you down.
- **Adjust in real-time.** Adjust in real-time according to how the audience responds and reacts to your speech.
- **Personalize.** You can personalize a speech by interacting with your audience.
- **Time.** You must manage your time. Monitor it and keep your speech flexible.
- **Space.** Think about how you will use your speaking area.

Questions (Q&A)

- **Repeat the question**
- **Answer the question!**
- **What if I don't know the answer?** Give the best answer you can and explain what you don't know. If possible, look to follow up with an answer after the event is over.
- **What if I don't get any questions?** Start by answering a question you often receive.

CHAPTER 5 - CONNECTION

These techniques will connect with your audience and make your speech great.

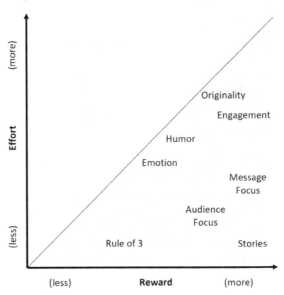

Speech Return on Investment (Speech ROI)

5.1 Stories

- **Why stories?** Everyone loves stories. Relive your own.
- **Tell a personal story.** You're the expert.
- **The basics:**
  - Who is in it? (Characters)
  - Where and when does it take place? (Setting)
  - What happens? (Plot)
- **Structure.** Have a clear beginning, middle, and end.
- **Dialogue.** Dialogue brings stories to life.
- **Characters.** Help the audience understand your characters by describing them and their motivations.

- **Don't be the hero of your own story.** Perhaps the hero is the person that helped you achieve your goal.
- **Present tense.** It's more exciting if you're able to relive stories in the present rather than the past.
- **Tension.** A story without tension or conflict is boring. Don't breeze over the moment toward an easy resolution. Can you heighten the tension?
- **Resolve questions.** Don't leave audience members with unresolved questions because this will distract and frustrate them.

5.2 Audience Focus

- **I vs. You.** Limit your use of "I" and focus on your audience by asking them questions.
- **Know your audience.** Adjust your message and delivery accordingly.
- **Tell the audience how they benefit.** Make the audience feel good about being there and keep them interested.
- **Don't alienate your audience.** Don't offend them or talk about something they have no interest in.

5.3 Message Focus

- **What do you want the audience to remember?** The more information you present, the more they will forget!
- **How can you get the audience to remember?**
    - Limit points.
    - Limit facts and statistics.
    - Emphasize, repeat and display key points.
    - Make key points memorable.
- **What do you want the audience to do?** Tell the audience what to do next and make it easy.
- **Translate facts and statistics.** Present facts and statistics in a way that means something to the audience.

5.4 Engagement

Take the audience from a passive to an active experience.

- **Curiosity:**
  - Ask a question. Tease the answer.
  - Start a story, then wait to reveal how it ends.
  - Show something new and create anticipation about how it works or what it does.
  - Reveal how the audience will benefit and get them excited about the results.
  - Reveal something surprising.
- **Demonstrations.** Demonstrations can bring an idea or product to life.
- **Participation.** Use questions, volunteers, whole audience participation, and electronic participation.

5.5 Originality

Being truly original guarantees that your audience will remember you and your speech.

- **Message.** Do you have a novel solution or approach to achieving your goal? Is your experience unusual, making you better qualified to deliver the message?
- **Stories.** What made your situation unusual, funny, or agony?
- **Person.** Do you have a characteristic that makes you stand out from other speakers or your audiences?
- **Presentation style and props.** Do you present in an unusual way or have unique props? What is your USP?

5.6 Humor

Humor is seeing the funny side of things.

- **Be self-deprecating.** Making fun of yourself works well as an icebreaker.
- **Common experience.** Mention something funny that you all experienced.

- **Funny observation.** See the funny side in situations.
- **Be emotional.** Strong emotions (overreacting) are funny.
- **Surprise.** A lot of humor is based on surprise.
- **Unintentional humor.** Any laugh is a good laugh.
- **When the audience laughs …** Allow them to finish laughing. If you can, build on the moment.

5.7 Emotion

- **Emotions beat logic.** Most people identify more with appeals to emotion.
- **Show the audience you care.** Use your emotions (especially passion and enthusiasm) when speaking.
- **Have fun.** Speaking is easier if you are having fun.
- **Tap into their memories.** Paint a scene in your audience's minds, and they'll fill it with their own images and memories.
- **Negative emotions.** Balance your speech so it has ups as well as downs.
- **Audiences remember how you made them feel, not what you said.**

5.8 Rule of Three

When we hear things in threes they are both pleasing to the ear and easy to remember.

CHAPTER 6 - ONLINE SPEAKING

6.1 Setup

- **Sound.** Your sound quality is most important. Test your microphone. Don't block it.
- **Video**
  - **Lighting.** Make sure you are lit in front of you (not behind) to see your face.
  - **Camera position.** Your camera should be in front of you and level with you so you are not looking up or down into it.
- **Environment.** Ideally, be somewhere quiet. Is your background clean and visually appealing?

6.2 Delivery

Presenting online

- **Eye contact.** Look into your webcam as if directly looking at your audience.
- **Energy.** Break up your presentation.

Online engagement

- Encourage cameras on.
- Use the chat feature, break-out rooms, quizzes, music, and video.

LAST
MINUTE
SPEAKING:

THE BOOK

INTRODUCTION
PRESENTATION PRIORITIES

Even if you are not an experienced speaker, you have probably heard lots of advice about how to give a speech and where to start.

"Start with a funny joke."
"Imagine the audience in their underwear!"
"Use note cards."
"Make lots of gestures."

It can be an overwhelming and lonely place. This book will change that. But the question remains, where do you start?

The Presentation Priorities Model

All the elements of public speaking can be placed in a logical order. These are shown in the Presentation Priorities Model. It is a bit like Maslow's Hierarchy of Needs but for speaking. Every speaker starts at the bottom. To progress to a higher level, you must pass through the lower levels. But, just because you have passed a certain level and moved up to the next level does not mean that you can forget about the lower levels. To be successful at the higher levels you need to maintain what you have achieved at the lower levels.

For example, confidence is something that you need to work on and maintain throughout the entire process of preparing, practicing, and delivering your speech. This means there may be times when you need to go back down and revisit a lower level. Even if you speak often, you will still be going through each of the Presentation Priorities levels each time you speak. The difference is that the more experienced you are, the easier the levels are to pass through.

Presentation Priorities Model

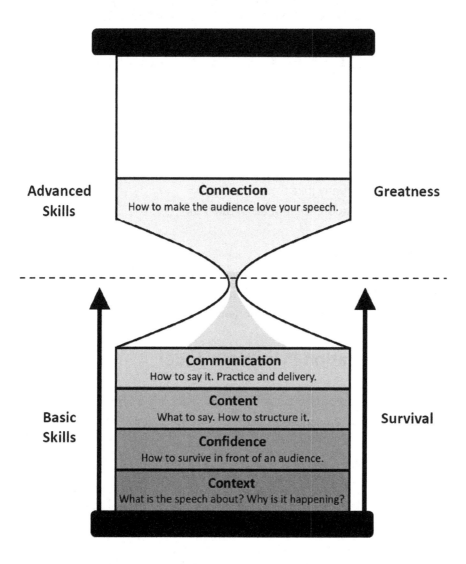

The Presentation Priorities Model is split into two main parts and five levels. The lower part forms the basic presentation skills and consists of four levels which make up the first four chapters of this book:

Basic Presentation Skills

Chapter 1 – Context: What are you speaking about and why are you speaking? This is your opportunity to get all the information you need to know before you go any further.

Chapter 2 – Confidence: Fear of public speaking is the biggest hurdle for many speakers and this can start long before the actual speech. This chapter will give you the confidence you need to prepare and speak successfully.

Chapter 3 – Content: What are you going to say? The best speeches have a clear structure and are easy to remember. Chapter 3 introduces you to the Speech Map - a new tool to help you complete your speaking journey without it feeling like a giant memory test.

Chapter 4 – Communication: Once you know what you are going to say, how are you going to say it? Assuming you are not giving your presentation in the next five minutes, you will want to practice. Chapter 4 shares some simple techniques both for useful practice and to deliver your speech well.

Advanced Presentation Skills

Everything you need to give a good presentation is covered in the first four chapters. However, if you are more ambitious and want to master advanced presentation skills then you can advance to the top of the Presentation Priorities Model.

Chapter 5 – Connection: The best speakers connect with their audience so that the audience fully understands their message and acts on it. Connection is achieved through masterful storytelling and engagement with the audience.

Specific Presentation Skills

The first five chapters apply generally to all types of speaking. However, you may be reading this book knowing that you have to give a specific type of speech. The following chapters give tips for more specific situations.

Chapter 6 – Online Speaking: Online speaking is now a mainstream way of presenting and allows you to reach audiences further afield than ever.

Chapter 7 – Specific Events: This chapter contains more specific information about work presentations, introductions and thank-you speeches, weddings, funerals, acceptance speeches, impromptu speaking, job interviews, local meetings, panel discussions, pitches, kids' and school presentations, competition debating, Toastmasters contests, and TED Talks.

CHAPTER 1
CONTEXT

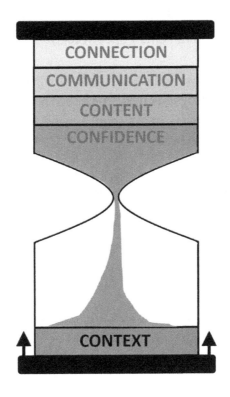

In this chapter...
1.1 Speech Requirements
1.2 Speech Logistics

The very first thing that you must do when asked to give a presentation is to understand the context of it. If you do not understand what the speech is about or even why it is happening, then you will not be able to prepare properly. This stage is very much the time to ask questions so that you understand as much as possible. By doing this, you will avoid wasting any time or energy and then be able to set off in the right direction. This will give you clarity which in turn will allow you to be much clearer when creating and delivering your presentation. All of this means that from the outset, you must understand the requirements of the speech you are to give and the logistics of the event.

Context = Speech Requirements + Speech Logistics

You can use the six main question words in English to understand the context of your speech. If you do not know the answers to these questions then you should find them out as soon as possible as they will help you create the best speech possible.

Speech Requirements

These are the background details you need to know that explain the speech that you will be giving.

What are you speaking about?
Why are **you** speaking?
Why is the speech happening?

Speech Logistics

These are all the details you need to know about the speech event itself.

When are you speaking?
Where are you speaking?
Who are you speaking to?
How are you speaking?

The Speech Context Questions diagram shows the importance of these questions, working from the center out to the corners.

Speech Context Questions

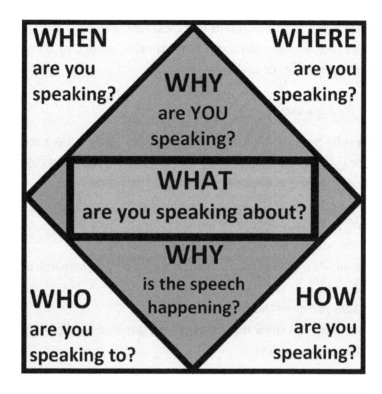

We will now consider each of these in order.

1.1 Speech Requirements

What Are You Speaking About?

This is the natural starting point because most speeches come about either by the speaker being asked to speak about a topic or the speaker proposing to speak about a topic:

- What type of speech are you giving? Is it a keynote presentation, lecture, workshop, etc.?
- Is the topic your choice or are you being told what to speak about?

- Do you understand the topic?
- Do you need to do more research on the topic?
- Are there any conventions you must follow for the type of speech you are giving? Chapter 7 lists specific points to consider for different types of speech.

Why Are YOU Speaking?

There must be a reason that makes sense of why **you** are the person who will be speaking. Understanding this will help you prepare your speech and also help your future audience know why you are speaking:

- Why were you chosen to speak?
- Why are you the right person to be speaking?
- Is this your area of responsibility (e.g., reporting research or results at work)?
- Have you done this before?
- What do you know that other people don't know about this topic?
- Are you an expert?

Why is the Speech Happening?

Your speech will most likely be connected to an event such as a conference, work report, group meeting, or special occasion. Each of these has different purposes, so understanding the event will help you understand what is required of your speech:

- What is the event or occasion you are speaking at?
- What is the purpose of that event or occasion?
- Within that event or occasion, what is the purpose of your speech?
- What will success look like (for you, the organizers, and the attendees)?

1.2 Speech Logistics

When Are You Speaking?

This affects how long you have to prepare your speech and how long your speech should be:

- On what date and time are you speaking?
- Are the date and time fixed or could they change?
- What time can you/should you show up at the event?
- How long are you speaking for? Is this fixed or is it flexible?
- Does the speech length include time for Q&A or is that outside it?
- Are there any deadlines before the event that you must meet (e.g., for submitting materials)?

Where Are You Speaking?

Not only is it necessary to know where you have to go to speak, but you will want to be able to get there in good time to prepare for delivering your speech:

- Where are you speaking (town, city, etc.)?
- Do you need to travel there?
- What travel arrangements must be made? Make sure you leave enough time to get there comfortably.
- Where are you speaking (venue building, room etc.)? Is it new to you or somewhere you know well?
- If the venue is new to you, when can you familiarize yourself with it?
- Who do you need to meet/talk to at the venue?

Who Are You Speaking To?

You have several people you must consider when creating and giving your speech:

- Who is your actual audience who will be sitting in front of you? What are they expecting from your speech? You may have to adjust your speech depending on this. For example, if your presentation was about a new product, a pitch to investors to raise money should be different from a selling demonstration to potential users.
- Who asked you or hired you to speak? What do they want to come out of your speech?
- What are the demographics of your audience? What are their: genders; ages; nationalities; professions?
- What is the expertise of your audience? Are you explaining new concepts from scratch to a general audience or are you speaking to a sophisticated, professional audience with a high level of understanding and experience?

How Are You Speaking?

The last general question to consider is how exactly you will be delivering your speech:

- Will you be at an in-person event or speaking online? Chapter 6 covers online speaking.
- What is the setup in the room where you will be speaking? How big is the room? Are you speaking from a stage? Is there a lectern for placing notes?
- Where will the audience be in the room? How will the audience be distributed (e.g., rows, tables)? How easily will they be able to see and hear you?
- What is the audiovisual equipment setup? Will you be wearing or using a microphone? Where will slides be displayed?
- Who can help you get set up to speak?
- Is there a dress code? What will you be wearing?
- Who will be introducing you?

One Final Note …

The context stage is how you should start preparing for your speech. It makes sense to gather as much information as possible so your preparation is focused in the right direction. Of course, any of the information mentioned in this chapter could change or be clarified as you get nearer to presenting your speech. Don't forget about the information in this chapter. You want to have it in your mind as you prepare and keep it as accurate and updated as possible.

CHAPTER 2
CONFIDENCE

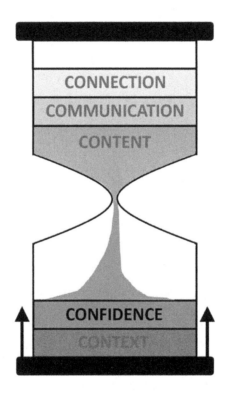

In this chapter...

Your heart probably started racing a little (or a lot) when you heard you were going to give a speech. Controlling your emotions is essential for effective speaking and your own wellbeing. So let's start with the elephant in the room.

2.1 Fear

The biggest hurdle for many new speakers is the fear of public speaking (or glossophobia to use its fancy name). It's often said public speaking is a bigger fear than death. No doubt the choice below is a challenge to many!

The fear of public speaking seems to act as an umbrella type of fear encompassing many other fears. When asked to explain their fear of speaking, most people usually list the following fears as reasons why they don't want to speak:

- Fear of being judged.
- Fear of making a mistake.
- Fear of looking stupid.

The antidote to fear is confidence. It is one of the most important parts of effective public speaking. Without confidence, it will be extremely difficult (if not impossible) to give your speech. Note that having confidence does not mean erasing all nerves. Even the best speakers have nerves when speaking. The key to nerves is to control them and channel the adrenaline they produce into energy that allows you to give the best speech possible in front of your audience.

The Speaker Nerves Spectrum

To help understand this, consider the Speaker Nerves Spectrum. Imagine that nervousness is a spectrum. At one end is a total, paralyzing fear of giving a speech. At the other end is complete apathy. Both are bad. If your fear is paralyzing, you will not be able to give your speech. But at the other end, if you are apathetic, you are almost too bored to give the speech. Because you don't care, you will just be going through the motions and your speech will not be its best.

There is an ideal middle ground between fear and apathy that you should aim for and that is excitement. If you are excited to give your speech then you will overcome your fear and find your motivation. Different approaches are needed to get to excitement depending on which end of the spectrum you find yourself starting on.

If you fear speaking, then you need to control it. The way to control it is through confidence which is what this chapter is about. At the apathy end, what you need to do is create energy to get yourself excited about speaking. When you are excited and speak, you should still have some nerves but they should be manageable. These nerves are what we often call nervous anticipation or butterflies in the stomach. This feeling will increase your alertness and presence in front of the audience, allowing you truly to speak in the moment and give the audience the best speech possible.

The Speaker Nerves Spectrum

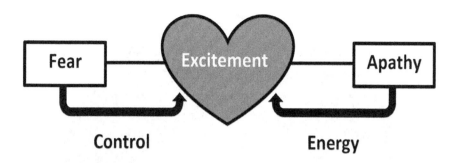

One final general point must be made about confidence. Although it is only the second level of Presentation Priorities, it needs to be sustained throughout the whole speech preparation and delivery effort. When you first find out that you are speaking, if you have confidence then you won't hope that the speech does not happen! Instead, you can focus on it as a reality and get on with the important work of creating, practicing, and delivering the best speech possible.

Confidence isn't universal either. You may have mastered it for speaking in front of certain audiences in certain settings but then find you need to acquire it again for a new speech in front of a new audience. Below are the tools and techniques to show you how to do this.

2.2 Mental Confidence

Confidence is mostly a mental issue and that means you need to work on it and control it from the moment you know you are going to give a speech. There are some physical aspects of confidence that are relevant at the actual time of giving a speech which I'll discuss in the next section. There are three key elements to gaining confidence and overcoming fear as shown in the following diagram.

The Secret to Confident Speaking

At the core, we see that the most important element is focusing on service to your audience. This is so fundamental that it forms a key part of the advanced skill of connecting to your audience too (see Chapter 5).

Outside that core element, there are two further elements of confidence that at first appear contradictory: (1) fake it till you make it and (2) the power of authenticity. These are represented by Yin and Yang in the diagram because although they appear to be opposites, they work together to complete your confidence. The challenge is in understanding how much of each you need at any moment and not using the wrong one at the wrong time.

Here is a quick summary of the main points of each of the three key elements of confidence. After this table, each element is explained in more detail.

The Secret to Confident Speaking

SERVICE TO YOUR AUDIENCE
- It's not about you - it's about them
- Be passionate about what you are speaking about
- Think of speaking as an opportunity, not an obligation
- Speaking is a privilege
- The audience wants you to succeed
- The audience needs to hear your message
- Think of the audience as individuals
- Your audience needs you to be a leader
- Be the expert and know your material

FAKE IT TILL YOU MAKE IT
- Visualize success
- Get on stage
- Visualize finishing
- Eliminate negative thoughts
- Show the audience you're in control
- Take control when speaking
- Get used to it but don't get over it

THE POWER OF AUTHENTICITY
- Authentic moments make the best connection
- Authentic moments are more memorable
- What's the worst that can happen?
- What if things go wrong?
- What if I blank out and forget everything?
- Be imperfect but not incompetent
- Failures are learning opportunities
- The value of humor
- Don't be afraid if you don't know the answer
- Don't be arrogant, but don't apologize
- Have fun

Service to Your Audience

Service to your audience means that you focus on them and their needs. What do they want? How will they benefit from your talk? How are they feeling right now? For example, an audience immediately after lunch might be quite lethargic. They might need to be woken up. Note that focusing on the audience does not mean "imagine them in their underwear!" This often-repeated piece of advice is a bad idea because it can only be a distraction.

It's Not About You - It's About Them

This is the single most useful piece of advice for becoming a confident speaker. Above, we broke down the fear of public speaking into fears of being judged, making a mistake, and looking stupid. All of these relate to you, the speaker. But the act of speaking is not about you. It's about your audience.

Example: My first day in court

I remember, as if it were yesterday, my first day alone in court as a new lawyer. I had my own client to defend. The seriousness of the occasion, the overwhelming responsibility on my shoulders, and my lack of experience were nearly a fatal combination. My client had been charged with multiple thefts and when I met him to take his instructions, I expected him to call me out immediately.

"Hey! You've never done this before have you?"
"Is this your first day?"
"Am I your first-ever case?"
"What makes you think you're qualified to represent me?"
"Do you know what you're doing?"
"What if you mess up?"
"Are you even old enough to be a lawyer?!" (I was only 23.)

Guess what? My client said none of these things! He only cared about himself. The reality and weight of the criminal proceedings against him were far more important to him than thinking about me. He needed my help. Not only did we both get through the hearing, but from that point on, it would never again be my first time.

In your audiences, everyone is living their own lives with their own problems. They are not worrying about you. When you stand up to speak, you have a chance to help them and change their lives for the better. So remember, it's not about you, it's about them!

There's a huge group of public speakers who have done an excellent job of internalizing the idea that it's not them but their audience that matters. These people are teachers. Every day their focus is on whether their students are learning and making progress. They don't have time to worry about what their students think of them. The only exception to this might be the very first day of school when a class is new and a teacher knows they're going to be making a first impression. There is a lesson here for every other public speaker to take from teachers. Make a great first impression with your audience and then quickly move on to concerning yourself about them, not you.

Interestingly, I've noticed that when teachers speak in front of adults (not their classes), many of them exhibit the usual fears of public speaking. Why? Because they fall back into the trap of worrying about what their audience thinks of them!

Be Passionate About What You Are Speaking About

If you love your topic or speech, that's great. If you don't, then you need to find a way to be more passionate about it. What can you share that is new, interesting, important, surprising, or funny? If you don't love your speech, neither will your audience.

Example: My speech in front of the whole school

My first love in life was castles. From about the age of five, I was obsessed with everything to do with knights and castles, battles and sieges. Most of my toys and books were about castles. You can imagine how excited I was when I started junior school (aged seven) and our very first class project was to build a model castle!

Every day at school started with all 400 children and teachers assembled in the main hall. Once a week, a different class would present their class project to the whole school. Eventually, it was time for my class to present our project. As we carefully carried our model castle down the hallway and into the hall, I looked up at my teacher and asked:

"Mrs. Quintrell?"
"Yes, Stuart."
"Who's going to tell everyone about our castle?"
"Well, I thought you could do that!"

She answered instantly! I'd had no warning. There was no time to prepare. Moments later, I was sitting on the stage looking out at the audience. 400 older faces stared back at me. I opened my mouth to speak and I'll never forget what happened next.

I absolutely loved it! I told the whole school all about the castle. I wanted them all to hear me so I spoke loudly and clearly. Mrs. Quintrell must have known what she was doing when she chose me to speak.

For years I felt very guilty about this story. I've met so many people who had a nightmare experience when they first spoke in front of an audience at school. For many, it put them off public speaking for life.

But when I reflected on this story, I realized something very important had happened when I stood on that stage all those years ago. This accidental discovery had protected me from the fear of public speaking.

I realized that I'd been so excited to talk about the castle, it had never even occurred to me to be nervous. I wanted to share my knowledge with everyone else so badly, I never considered what they might be thinking about me.

By sheer chance, I had discovered one of the most important rules of public speaking. You should be passionate about what you are speaking about.

Think of Speaking as an Opportunity, Not an Obligation

This is a subtle shift of thinking that is useful for anything in life that you don't want to do (not just speaking). Rather than feeling that you have to speak against your will, it is better to think that you have been given an opportunity to speak that you are choosing to take. In simple terms, think "today I **GET** to speak" rather than "today I **HAVE** to speak." What is the opportunity? It can be many things such as:

- An opportunity to share an important message with your audience.
- An opportunity to change or improve people's lives.
- An opportunity for personal growth.

Choice is empowering, so even if speaking wasn't originally your choice, your confidence will improve if you make it your choice to be there.

Speaking is a Privilege

This builds on the previous point. Speaking is not just an opportunity but also a privilege. We all have limited time on earth and your audience is choosing to listen to you. If you speak to 100 people for 30 minutes that is 50 hours of audience listening time and it only took you 30 minutes to deliver. What a great way to amplify your influence and impact! This means that, as the speaker, you have great power to choose what you say, but also great responsibility not to waste the audience's time.

The Audience Wants You to Succeed

Think about any time you've gone to a concert or form of entertainment. You don't want to be disappointed. You want it to be amazing. Believe it or not, this is the best outcome for your audience too.

Not all people in an audience may have voluntarily chosen to be there but the fact is that they're there now. In these circumstances, the best thing for them is to be pleasantly surprised by how good you are and how useful your message is. In other words, they also want you to succeed.

The Audience Needs to Hear Your Message

If your message is valuable (see Chapter 3), then the audience needs to hear it. If you do not speak or share your message then you are depriving them of something to help them or improve their lives.

Think of the Audience as Individuals

It can be intimidating thinking about a large audience so it is better to think of them as individuals. Each person has their own problems and struggles in life and is listening to you speak for a reason. Your message only needs to resonate with one person in the audience for it to be worthwhile. Similarly, remember you can't please everyone. Focus instead on the individuals who need your message.

When speaking, try to find the friendlier faces in the room that seem to be receptive to your message (by smiling and nodding). Use these people as mental support while speaking. Interestingly, while it can be helpful to avoid unfriendly faces, you should not assume their expressions are a judgment on your speech. There might be any number of reasons why a person's face is not smiling that has nothing to do with what you are saying. Every speaker I know has a story about an audience member that they thought hated their speech because of their facial expressions but who later revealed how much they appreciated it.

While audiences are made up of individuals that are human and vulnerable, it is not good advice to "imagine them in their underwear." If that were even possible, it would only be a distraction!

Thinking of the audience as individuals overlaps with connection to your audience. In Chapter 5, we discuss that you should also speak to your audience as individuals because your message will seem more personalized and relevant to them.

Your Audience Needs You to be a Leader

Sometimes you might find yourself speaking to audience members who could have been speaking instead. Perhaps you volunteered (or were voluntold by your boss). Most of the audience would not like to be in your position so this is your chance to be a leader. Someone has to present this important information and it might as well be you!

Be the Expert and Know Your Material

In Chapter 3, we examine Speech Maps which set out the message and direction of your speech very clearly. By the time you have created your Speech Map, you will have a very clear idea of what you are going to say to your audience and your confidence should grow. You won't be panicking because you don't know what to say.

Introducing Faking It and Authenticity

Service to your audience is by far the most important aspect of increasing your confidence because it takes the attention off yourself and demands you focus on the important mission of improving your audience's lives.

Sometimes though, there will be smaller moments that will test your confidence and you must decide what to do. There are two techniques to use but the problem is that they appear to be contradictory: faking it and being authentic.

Faking it can boost your confidence because you create the image or illusion that you are more confident and experienced than you are. This improves both your own state of mind and the audience's confidence in you which loops in a virtuous circle to continue growing your confidence.

Being authentic can boost confidence because you show that you are comfortable with who you are and the situation you are in. The audience appreciates that you are real and there for them which boosts their confidence in you. At the end of this section, we will look at how you might choose which works best, but first, let's understand how faking it and authenticity work.

Fake It Till You Make It

The following different ways of faking it are important for your success. As you get more used to using them, you can use them as "experience" rather than thinking about "faking it."

Visualize Success

It is absolutely critical that you imagine yourself speaking successfully. This is exactly the same as the focus and positive thinking that great athletes use for success in their sports. There are lots of things you can do to help this visualization. In Chapter 1 (Context), you identified all the key information you needed about your presentation. Now visualize it:

- Visualize yourself traveling to the venue.
- Visualize giving the speech.
- Visualize being on stage or in the room you will be in.
- Visualize looking at the audience.
- Visualize yourself answering questions.
- Visualize how great you will feel at the end of your successful speech.

The more you can visualize, the more familiar it will become. In the future, you can use your past successes to help visualize your future ones. Even if the experience, venue, or audience are new, they will seem more familiar when the time comes because you visualized them.

Get on Stage

One of the most important aspects of visualizing is to go to the actual place you are speaking and imagine giving the speech. If there is a stage, actually get on it at any point before the presentation and imagine giving your presentation. This might be the night before in an empty room at a conference or even during an interval between other presentations. When the time comes to deliver your presentation, being on the stage will seem more familiar to you.

When you check out the room and stage where you are speaking, be sure to check out the different parts of the room where your audience will be sitting. What will it be like for them? Will they be able to see and hear you? This focus on the audience will help you deliver your speech better for them when the time comes.

Visualize Finishing

If you are nervous about speaking, perhaps the most comforting thing to visualize is finishing your speech and walking off. Imagine something nice that you will be doing afterward, whether it is going home to a loved one or having a drink. You know for certain that such a moment will come and that when it comes, you will have delivered your speech! Imagine how great and relaxed you will feel at that moment. You can then think of your presentation as a step toward that enjoyable moment. Another advantage to visualizing finishing is that as the speech gets closer, so does the finishing time.

> Don't think: "Arggh! Only one hour until I speak!"
> Think: "Great! In just two hours I'll be finished and going home!"

Eliminate Negative Thoughts

There is one final point to make about visualization. We have seen how thoughts can be self-fulfilling. That is why it is all the more important to have positive thoughts to reinforce the idea that you will be successful. If instead, you think negatively ("I'm going to forget my speech and look stupid"), you increase the chances of that happening. Try to recognize when your brain is filling your head with negative thoughts so that you can start ignoring them or, better still, reframing them. If I have to walk across a narrow balance beam and tell myself, "I'm going to fall," I will almost certainly fall. Instead, I need to tell myself, "I can do this!"

Show the Audience You're in Control

This is very important! As a speaker, the best gift you can give the audience is to be calm and in control, regardless of what you are actually feeling inside. Watching a speaker struggle is a painful, cringeworthy experience. The audience instead wants to know it can relax and enjoy the talk because the speaker is confident in what they have to share. If the audience can't relax, they can't take in what you are saying.

Example: The pilot

The role of a speaker is a lot like a pilot. Imagine if you sat down on a plane and heard this:

"Er … good morning … ladies and gentlemen. Er, this is your Captain speaking. I've never actually done this before so bear with me while we get started. I'm just trying to figure out how to switch this thing on. So today, we're going to … hang on a minute … we're going to … New York, I think. I'm not sure how long it's going to take, but hopefully, we'll get most of the way there. I'm sure most of you know more than I do so I apologize if I make any mistakes. Anyway, sit back and hopefully, this flight won't go wrong!"

Most of the passengers would be rushing for the exits! But why do so many speakers start in a similarly nervous and apologetic way? Don't make your audience run for the exits!

One of the biggest clichés about public speaking on TV and in movies is the speaker awkwardly forgetting their speech. I hate this! Not only does it reinforce the idea that speaking is impossibly hard but it also makes it incredibly awkward to watch, especially if it is real (such as on the TV show *Shark Tank*).

You will probably have some nerves when speaking, just as a new pilot might. As the Speaker Nerves Spectrum diagram showed, by controlling those nerves (for example, by hiding them from the audience) you can boost your confidence and channel the nerves into excitement.

Take Control When Speaking

There are other ways you can show you are in control when speaking. You can adjust what you are saying for the audience's benefit. You can choose to answer questions. You can react spontaneously to something that happens. You can choose when a break might happen or when to break up your speech (perhaps by doing something interactive). All these little decisions, subtly reinforce that the audience is in your control and they will thank you for it.

Get Used to it but Don't get Over it

As you get more used to public speaking, there is a great relief to know that you can do it. The more you do it, the more your muscle memory kicks in and the experience becomes familiar to you, just like driving a car. Use this feeling any time you doubt yourself: "I may feel nervous today, but I know that tomorrow I'll go out there and give a great speech!" Remind yourself that you've done this before and that any nerves are normal and you can channel them toward excitement. The one thing to avoid is getting so used to it that you've started to get over this whole speaking thing. You do not want to suppress all your nerves as you will then risk being at the apathy end of the spectrum.

A Note for Introverts

I understand that much of the idea of faking it can be uncomfortable for introverts. Public speaking can often seem like an activity for outgoing people who like to show off. There is a way in which public speaking is great for introverts though. The stage is a safe place that you control. That means you can predict what will happen during your presentation in a way you cannot if you are meeting other people in the normal course of work or a social setting. I count myself among many speakers who say they are more introverted than extroverted. If you do too, try to see the stage as a safe place for you.

The Power of Authenticity

Authentic Moments Make the Best Connection

No matter how experienced you are, an authentic moment presents a unique opportunity to have a special connection with your audience. In such moments, your audience won't want to be anywhere else.

Example: Turning despair into hope

Many years ago, I attended a talk by comedian Judy Carter. Judy's presentation had been going very well when she was asked a difficult question by a woman in the audience who had experienced a very traumatic event in her life. The questioner wanted to know how she could possibly apply Judy's advice to her own tragic, personal situation. The atmosphere in the room became electric with uncertainty and anticipation. Everyone sensed that the success of Judy's presentation depended on her ability to answer this question.

She paused to think because she had clearly not anticipated this question and therefore, her answer was not one that she could have previously prepared. After careful reflection, Judy shared something personal and meaningful about her own life that led her to conclude that the questioner had a valuable experience and message of her own to share with people. The woman gratefully appreciated this advice and many tears were shed.

If Judy had tried to give a generic answer, she would not have been successful. Instead, she created an unforgettable moment where her authenticity saved the day. The reason it worked so well is that in that moment it was clear that Judy cared about nothing other than helping this questioner with her situation. Judy's authenticity and advice made an amazing connection between her and everyone in the room.

Authentic Moments are More Memorable

I once watched an interview presentation between two speakers who had prepared and rehearsed together. The first few minutes proceeded smoothly and uneventfully. Then one of the speakers asked a question and the other person forgot the answer they had prepared. The second speaker didn't panic but was honest instead. The moment was funny and it was also the point when the presentation came alive. From that point both the speakers became real people, not flawless robots and the audience appreciated it a lot more.

What's the Worst That Can Happen?

Part of being authentic is also being honest and realistic. New speakers can have a habit of catastrophizing what will happen when they speak. The brain kicks in with a fight or flight response and they imagine the worst possible outcomes such as forgetting everything, embarrassing themselves, and maybe losing a job or some similar setback. But it's worth being realistic when asking, "What's the worst that can happen?" Remember, there is no physical threat in speaking. You're not going to be attacked! Most of the time the answer should be that there is not much of great consequence riding on your speech. Your speech doesn't define your self-worth or value as a person. Regardless of how your speech goes, life will still go on and you will be OK. Try to keep that perspective when speaking. Even if something goes wrong, it's not the end of the world!

What If Things Go Wrong?

So, what if something does go wrong? Two solutions to this are planning and perspective. Planning means anticipating as much as possible in advance that could go wrong. If you are using technology, what happens if it doesn't work? Can you give your speech without slides or a microphone? If you have anticipated these problems, then aside from hopefully preventing them, if they do occur you will be able to act authentically and reasonably in the moment and the organizers and audience will appreciate that.

Perspective is necessary when something occurs that maybe you did not foresee. If you have been diligent and done your best, you should not worry that something went wrong. Organizers may be panicking too so the best thing you can do is be a calm, professional leader who can help them. If you do or say something that is unexpectedly funny, enjoy it. Don't be embarrassed. I always consider it an achievement if I can make people laugh, no matter how it's done. Every speaker knows that one silver lining with anything going wrong is that it instantly becomes a story to use in future speeches. Sharing your failures or embarrassments is authentic and will make you more human and likable.

What If I Blank Out and Forget Everything?

This is a dramatic scenario that will not happen, but I'm including it here because it is such a common fear. First, don't panic, and remember to breathe. If you forget your next point but can continue, then do so. The chances are that you will remember what you wanted to say and can just add it in seamlessly later. The audience will never know.

If you have a worse moment where your mind goes completely blank, again, don't panic and keep breathing. There are lots of things you can do to get back to where you were. In Chapter 3, you will see that ideally, you should have a Speech Map outlining your speech rather than a script. This means that you should have internalized your overall message and key points instead of trying to remember the text of a speech. By remembering the Speech Map and using it to think about your overall message and key points along the way, you might be able to remember where you were and continue speaking. If the audience is small, you could even ask them, "Where was I?" which shows them your authenticity.

Failing that, you should have a useful copy of your Speech Map with you (on your person or a table or lectern). A useful copy means it is a useful outline of your speech, that allows you to glance at it and get back to where you were. Even if you rely on a fully written out script, you should still have a Speech Map of it so you can quickly identify where you were when you got lost. Chapter 3 discusses Speech Maps in detail. I also discuss a similar experience I had with what I call my hijacking brain in the section on the curse of the script.

Be Imperfect but Not Incompetent

This is an important distinction to understand. Everyone makes mistakes. No one is perfect and pretending to be perfect as a speaker will only alienate you from your audience. Not only that but, as the saying goes, if your goal is to be perfect you are doomed to failure. However, as a speaker, you should be competent. That means you should have put in the preparation, planning, and practice necessary to be able to deliver your speech. Acknowledging an honest mistake when speaking is fine. But blundering through a speech where you don't seem to know what you are doing is not OK.

Failures are Learning Opportunities

Many speakers I know have the mindset that when something bad or embarrassing happens to them, these are not just learning opportunities but also great stories and examples for future speeches. These failures might occur in speeches themselves or just in life generally. The great thing about this positive way of thinking is that it inoculates you from fearing failure.

The Value of Humor

I'm a big fan of humor and think it is appropriate in just about every speech. Making an audience laugh connects them to you. Unless you are a comedian, it is also a pleasant surprise to them as they will not necessarily be expecting to laugh. Humor can be deliberate or unexpected. If something unexpected and funny happens, it is important that you can authentically accept it. If you do, you show you're in control and essentially you're giving the audience permission to laugh. If however, you try to ignore it or deny it, the situation might become awkward and the audience might cringe.

Don't be Afraid if You Don't Know the Answer

We seem to be living in an age where many leaders are happy to say anything or make up answers to things they don't know. Do not do this! Your credibility as a speaker and expert on your topic is at stake. It is fine to say that you don't know the answer to a question and will either find out or offer an educated opinion as an answer. No one knows everything and often the essence of being a professional expert is that you know how to find answers rather than having them all at your fingertips.

Don't be Arrogant, but Don't Apologize

Confidence is the middle ground. You are not better than the audience so don't be arrogant. On the other hand, you are not worse than your audience so don't apologize to them. You want them to relate to you, not feel sorry for you. One of the worst ways a speaker can start a speech is, "I'm sorry you have to listen to me today." If you truly feel that way then why should the audience listen to you? On the other hand, if you are being insincere, that is not authentic.

Have Fun

The difference between a speaker who is having fun and enjoying themselves and a speaker who is merely undertaking their job is very obvious to an audience. Speaking can be fun for lots of reasons. It's fun to interact with people and change their lives for the better. It's fun to go to new places or make people laugh. If you are having fun, your audience will too.

Example: How my friend Ed used fun to get me speaking again

In the summer of 2012, I stopped speaking in public. The reason was that I'd found out I was getting divorced and it felt like my life was falling apart. I couldn't find the energy or interest to speak, let alone to do it well.

One Sunday, I spent a day in Rhode Island with my friend Ed Skurka and I finally started practicing public speaking again. During that day with Ed, we did many different speaking exercises. Some were silly. Some took me outside my comfort zone. All of them gave me energy. I rediscovered how much fun speaking is and how much easier speaking is when you are having fun.

Less than a week later, I stood on a stage in front of 2,000 people and came third in the Toastmasters World Championship of Public Speaking! I will forever be grateful to Ed for that lesson that ended up changing my life.

How do You Choose Between Faking It and Authenticity?

As a speaker there are endless situations you might be faced with, so how should you decide between faking it and being authentic at any given moment? There is no universal answer to this, but the key factor to ask yourself is, **"What will make the audience's experience better?"** This should not come as a surprise, because that is our central element for being confident.

The audience's experience will be improved by anything which makes them:

- better understand your material
- connect with you
- laugh

The audience's experience will be worsened by anything which makes them:

- annoyed
- confused
- bored

The table below shows a few examples of how this might work.

Fake It or Be Authentic?
You feel underprepared
Fake It: You hide your feelings and continue as if everything is normal. The audience doesn't notice you feel underprepared.
Be Authentic: You reveal how underprepared you feel. The audience wonders why they should listen to you and may feel insulted you didn't prepare properly and are wasting their time.
Solution: Fake It
Your slide presentation doesn't work
Fake It: If you try to pretend everything is normal as you get continued error messages, the audience will think you are incompetent.
Be Authentic: If you are honest about the technology not working and move on without it, the audience will appreciate your flexibility.
Solution: Be Authentic
There is a loud distraction in the room
Fake It: You try to ignore the distraction but it continues. Some of the audience members are more focused on it than they are on you and you start to lose them.

Be Authentic: Acknowledge the distraction (the "elephant in the room") as it will make the audience realize you are thinking just like they are. They will have a stronger connection to you.

Solution: Be Authentic

You forget something you wished to say

Fake It: Carry on without it or work it in at a later stage.

Be Authentic: Acknowledge that you have something to add to what you said earlier.

Solution: Be Authentic *or* Fake It

You say or do something unintentionally funny

Fake It: Pretend it didn't happen. The situation might become awkward, especially if the audience feels unable to enjoy the funny moment.

Be Authentic: Go with the flow and appreciate the audience's laughter. Build on the humor if you can.

Solution: Be Authentic

You don't know the answer to a question

Fake It: Make up an answer. Hope that it doesn't get fact-checked and the audience can't tell you're faking. If they find out, your credibility will be damaged.

Be Authentic: Acknowledge the reality that you don't know. Offer your best advice or find an answer after the presentation. The audience will appreciate you being as helpful as you can.

Solution: Be Authentic

2.3 Physical Confidence

Mental confidence is important because your mind is always with you. From the moment you know you will be speaking, you must prepare yourself mentally. But as you get closer to the actual moment of speaking, you must also prepare your physical confidence.

Your Body's Basics

You have been doing all of the following since you were born. However, you should give them some thought before speaking so that they help your confidence and don't hinder it.

- **Sleep** – Make sure you are well rested, especially before speaking. Though your body will naturally create adrenalin for when you are presenting, you still want to be as alert as you can. If you find that your mind is active the night before speaking and you can't sleep, resting with your eyes closed (and rehearsing mentally) is better than nothing.
- **Breathing** – Slow, deep breathing can help calm you. It is even more effective if you can find a quiet place outside to reflect calmly.
- **Food** – Digesting food consumes energy and feeling full can make you sluggish. If you want to eat before speaking, it should be far enough in advance that it will not interfere with your energy levels. Generally, I prefer to speak on a relatively empty stomach and eat afterward.
- **Drink** – Water is the best drink and you should have some nearby when speaking. Caffeine drinks have the advantage of waking you up and boosting your energy but can also be dehydrating. Use your knowledge of your own body to know what works best for you. Remember that you will not want to be making a bathroom break while speaking.
- **Clothing** – Wear clothing and shoes that are appropriate but also comfortable. Practice speaking in this clothing. I nearly fainted

once when speaking because my tie and collar were too tight and were choking me! If you will be using a microphone such as a lavalier (that clips to your clothing), make sure that you have somewhere to clip it and somewhere to attach the transmitter.

Walking

Walking is a wonderful practice that can both get your blood flowing and energy levels up while simultaneously calming your nerves. If at all possible, try to walk a bit before speaking.

Practice, Practice, Practice

Practice is discussed in Chapter 4. The more you do it the easier it gets (like exercise). Remember that you are not just practicing the content of your speech but also timing, movement, using technology, and so on. Practice improves your muscle memory which means when you give your speech it will be more familiar to you.

Get Used to Yourself

Everyone has experienced the shock of hearing their own voice on a recording for the first time. It sounds different because the sound of your voice travels to you through your bones and the air. Your audience (or any recording device) only hears the sound of your voice through the air. The bad news is that unfortunately, no one else in the world will ever get to hear how beautiful and resonant your voice sounds as it does to you when you hear yourself speak. The good news is that everyone else has only ever heard your voice as it actually sounds and they have already accepted it and got used to it. So should you! My voice still sounds better in my head than how other people hear it, but at least I've accepted it now. This advice also applies to how you look.

One way to get used to yourself is to record yourself and watch it back. You may cringe at first, but after a while, you'll get used to it. It's also a great way to evaluate and improve your speaking. Remember, if you see something you don't like, the audience sees it too. Why should they have to listen to something you don't want to? We owe it to our audiences to get better.

Routine

If it helps, you can develop a routine before speaking. For me, I mainly focus on the basics mentioned above and also looking at the outline of my speech. Other people listen to music. Motivational speaker Tony Robbins bounces on a mini trampoline before speaking which increases his energy. You can also warm up your vocal cords. Sometimes, I will hum quietly as this can even work in a crowded room without people noticing.

Your Presentation Begins When You Can be Seen

Your presentation starts the moment that your audience first sees you (not when you start speaking). It took me a long time to realize this. The mistake I used to make was thinking that the need for confident body language only started when I began speaking and not before. As a result, I would modestly approach the stage and the introvert in me avoided eye contact with the audience. I then noticed that other speakers projected confidence as soon as they were introduced.

Example: The pilot again

Earlier on we compared a speaker to a pilot. Imagine if you saw a trembling wreck of a pilot as you boarded the plane, but he later sounded confident as he introduced himself on the intercom. You would still be uncomfortable wouldn't you? The same applies here. You must project confidence at all times to maximize your audience's comfort.

When you are first visible to your audience might vary. It could be as you are introduced to speak, when the audience is entering the room, or even the night before, mingling at a conference. If you are presenting to your boss at work in the afternoon but you see him in the morning, your presentation has begun and you need to project confidence.

Body Language

"Power poses" seem very artificial to me but I do think body language is important when speaking. What does confident body language look like? Rather than encourage an unnatural power pose, I'd rather ask the question what does confident body language **not** look like? Don't do anything that suggests you are embarrassed or apologetic for being there. In other words, don't hunch over or avoid looking at people, and especially don't run off stage at the end of your speech. Stand up straight, look people in the eyes and move purposefully on stage. You are worthy to be speaking and you are there for a reason. You have a job to do and it's going to make people's lives better. They're lucky to have you and you are going to have a good time.

Voice

When you are on stage, your voice can project confidence that you might not be feeling inside. Speaking clearly and projecting your voice so that all of your audience can hear you are important delivery skills but they also help your confidence.

Example: My surprisingly confident voice

In some of my early speeches, I remember being surprised by the confident sound of my voice when I started speaking on stage. It was as if the bold voice and the insecure, shy brain were disconnected.

"Wow! He sounds confident," I thought. Gradually I learned that voice really was mine and I owned it.

2.4 Energy

From Apathy to Excitement

The majority of this chapter has focused on speakers who are at the "fear" end of the Speaker Nerves Spectrum because that is a far more common problem. If you are at the "apathy" end of the spectrum, it probably means you are a much more experienced speaker. The danger here is that you have given the same presentation to different audiences or spoken to the same audience about different topics and any excitement you once had has been replaced with overfamiliarity or apathy. The good news is that it is easier to move from apathy to excitement because you should not have the self-doubt which can paralyze the new, fearful speaker at the other end of the spectrum. You have probably been at the excitement part of the spectrum before and you know you can be there again. Here are some ways you can generate energy to make you more excited about speaking.

Change Your Speech

The most obvious step to take is to change your speech. It does not need to be a large or dramatic change. Finding just one new story or a piece of humor can give you the excitement you need to look forward to giving a speech and seeing how an audience reacts. In any case, best practice should mean that you are always looking to improve your speech. You can identify the weakest section and look to replace it or improve it. Sometimes you can get a sense that even a good part of a speech could work better than it does already. Each time you improve it, you get a chance to test it on an audience, which is exciting.

Make Your Speech More Interactive

One of the dangers with a bored speaker is that the audience's energy is likely to match the speaker's own. Conversely, if you can get the audience engaged and excited about your speech then their energy will flow to you. Even if you are giving a keynote speech (rather than a workshop), there are ways to get the audience involved.

- **Questions** – Ask the audience questions. If rhetorical, give them time to think and answer in their heads. If you don't want a verbal response, you can still get them to raise their hands ("yes" or "no") or even use smartphone apps to answer questions you have already created. If you are answering an audience member's question, you also create the excitement of giving a spontaneous answer.

- **Exercises** – Exercises can break up the flow of just hearing the speaker speak. You can get audience members to work individually, in pairs, or in groups. I once had the privilege of being in an audience where the speaker turned us into an orchestra making sound using any objects we had on us. He then split us into four sections and conducted us as we spontaneously created and performed a musical piece about our surroundings - "The Symphony of the Lecture Hall."

- **Humor** – In my experience, people always like to laugh and be entertained. Even some of our darkest moments in life are often not far from humor as in, "I didn't know whether to laugh or cry." If you can make an audience laugh, they will usually appreciate it. The best way to do this is not by telling jokes, but rather to tell stories where funny things happened or describe situations where you observed something funny. Self-deprecating humor usually works very well too. For more about humor, see Chapter 5.6.

Overall, the key message here is to have fun and be playful. Remember that more audience energy will give you more energy.

Find Things to Look Forward to

An important part of creating energy is to find something about the speaking experience that you are looking forward to. This could be a change to your speech or the interactivity mentioned above. It could also be a favorite part of your speech such as a signature story that always gets a great reaction. It could be surprising people by doing something different and unexpected. It might be the satisfaction of presenting a complicated or technical idea in simple terms that can easily be understood. There might also be other things to look forward to that are not necessarily about the speaking itself. Maybe you will enjoy meeting new people, making new contacts, or traveling to a new place.

Think About the Importance of Your Message

On some level, your message must be really important. If you are a motivational speaker, your message has a chance to change people's lives. That is urgent and exciting business. Even if you have less control over your speech (e.g., your boss has asked you to present the quarterly reports) you still have a chance to make a difference, by highlighting and analyzing important information on which future decisions will be made. Speaking gives you power and influence which are privileges to use wisely but also be excited about.

Change Your Motivation

Sometimes you can pretend your speech is something that it is not. Before delivering a speech, Toastmasters World Champion Darren LaCroix recommends asking yourself, "How would I give this speech if I knew it was my last one ever?" This can help create a sense of urgency and presence that you might not otherwise have.

Change Your Audience

This might not be an option for you depending on your circumstances, but you might be able to find different audiences or organizations for your speeches. This can turn speaking back into a learning experience for you as you discover how different audiences react to your message. If you are a Toastmaster, try visiting and speaking at different clubs to give yourself more variety.

Create Fear!

Be careful with this suggestion. I can't say I recommend it, but it might work for you. If you are a procrastinator at heart, you may find that you can use an approaching speaking deadline to adrenalize yourself. A (controlled) sense of panic as the moment gets closer and more real can help give you energy to focus on creating and delivering a speech.

Please note though that it is always better to be well prepared. The general theme of this book is that even though there are many things you can do to create a successful speech at the last minute, the longer you have, the better you can make your speech.

Physical Energy Before Speaking

There are various ways to create energy before you go on stage. Any activity that gets your blood flowing (but doesn't exhaust you) can be good. Even jumping up and down on the spot a few times can create some energy. You can also use positive self-talk or motivating music to get you in the right frame of mind. As a general rule, it is a good idea to start your presentation with higher energy as that is when you are making your first impression and the people in the audience are deciding if they are interested in what you have to say or not.

2.5 Speaker Types

From everything we have learned in this chapter, it is possible to see that there are four types of speakers based on two variables:

- Are you confident or unconfident?
- Do you focus on your audience or yourself?

The tables on the next page show these different speaker types. Do not worry if you are a beginner. Everyone starts here, but hopefully, this chapter has shown you how to develop the confidence to move past this stage. You will realize from these tables that focusing on your audience is crucial. We saw from the secret to confident speaking diagram that service to your audience lies at the core of being a confident speaker. It is also essential for becoming a good speaker.

What's your Speaker Type?

> ### Unconfident + Focus on Self = THE BEGINNER
>
> Everyone starts here. The thought of speaking in front of an audience is initially so terrifying that you can only think about yourself and what people will think of you. You might feel "imposter syndrome" or be tempted to hide behind lots of slides. Don't worry – read this book!

> ### Unconfident + Focus on Audience = THE DEVELOPING SPEAKER
>
> This speaker wants to provide value to their audience but is still learning to feel comfortable doing it. Work on improving your confidence so that it doesn't hold you back and limit your value to audiences. Practice and experience will make this easier!

> ### Confident + Focus on Self = THE WINDBAG
>
> A speaker who likes the sound of their own voice or does not put the audience first by giving them what they need. If there are slides, they may go on forever. How can you focus your message so that you only tell the most important parts?

> ### Confident + Focus on Audience = THE ORATOR
>
> A powerful speaker who knows they have a valuable message to share and who connects with their audience. Never stop improving!

There is only one category of speaker that is unacceptable – the windbag! You will surely have had the misfortune of suffering through a speech by such a speaker. All you can do is look at the time and wonder when it will be over. Once you've developed your confidence, you only have two choices: be an orator or a windbag. Please don't be a windbag!

CHAPTER 3
CONTENT

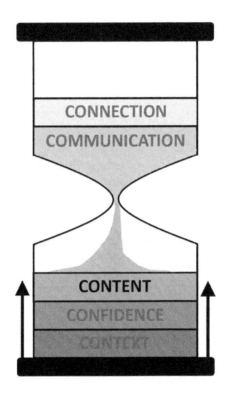

In this chapter...

3.1 Speech Purpose – Why Are You Speaking?

3.2 Speech Topic – What Are You Speaking About?

3.3 Speech Maps – How Do You Structure Your Speech?

3.4 Speech Materials – What Else Do You Need for Your Presentation?

Once you have got all the information you need to speak (see Chapter 1) and armed yourself with the tools to be confident (see Chapter 2) you are ready to create your speech. There are two key elements to a good speech: content and delivery. This chapter will focus on the content of your speech and how to structure it in the best way. Chapter 4 will show you how to practice and deliver your speech well.

3.1 Speech Purpose – Why Are You Speaking?

When your speech preparation started and you went through the context stage of preparing for your speech (Chapter 1), you should have got a clear idea of why you are speaking. Nevertheless, as you create the content for your speech, it is time to think a little more about the purpose of your speech.

It is often said that there are three different purposes for speaking: to persuade, to inform, or to entertain. To better understand their speech content, speakers are encouraged to identify which type of speech they are giving.

- **PERSUASIVE** - Is the speech trying to convince the audience that a particular point of view is correct or to change their minds?
- **INFORMATIVE** - Is the speech designed to educate the audience by telling them something new or telling them how to do something?
- **ENTERTAINING** - Is the factual content of the speech secondary to the fact that the audience members enjoy themselves and have a good time?

At school, students learn the same purposes exist for writing and they are often encouraged to remember the acronym "PIE" (Persuasive, Informative, Entertaining). We might think of this in diagram form as follows:

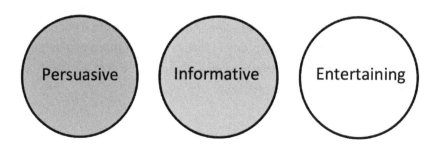

I believe this is wrong! It is my view that the vast majority of speeches should have all three PIE purposes in them. The reason for this is that each speech purpose complements the others. Even if a speech has a primary purpose, it will be as appealing and effective as possible if it includes all three purposes. The following tables show how and why you can do this.

PERSUASIVE SPEAKING
How can you achieve this? Use a mixture of appealing to the audience's logic and emotion. Emphasize your credibility.
How does this speech purpose benefit an INFORMATIVE Speech? Usually, an informative speech is more than just an indifferent presentation of information. A speaker typically wishes to persuade their audience to change their views or take action based on the information. This requires persuasion.
How does this speech purpose benefit an ENTERTAINING Speech? Entertaining an audience starts with persuading them to accept what you are saying or doing. Comedians often do this by identifying common ground or emotions with their audience and then sharing relevant experiences with them.

INFORMATIVE SPEAKING

How can you achieve this?
Present a range of interesting, relevant information. Give examples and illustrations to make it easy to understand.

How does this speech purpose benefit a PERSUASIVE Speech?
Facts and information will support your argument. Be careful not to misrepresent them or to overwhelm the audience with too many facts and statistics though.

How does this speech purpose benefit an ENTERTAINING Speech?
While entertaining is a valid goal in its own right, an audience benefits even more if they feel they learned something along the way. This makes them feel their time spent was not just fun but productive too.

ENTERTAINING SPEAKING

How can you achieve this?
Demonstrate a talent, humor, or something surprising or unusual. Be interactive with the audience.

How does this speech purpose benefit a PERSUASIVE Speech?
If the audience is entertained, they will enjoy the speech and pay better attention to it. Presenting with humor will make it easier to remember your arguments.

How does this speech purpose benefit an INFORMATIVE Speech?
If the audience is entertained, they will enjoy the speech and pay better attention to it. TED talks are primarily informative, but often very entertaining. Learning new things is entertaining for a curious person.

We can more accurately represent the connection between speech purposes as the following Venn diagram.

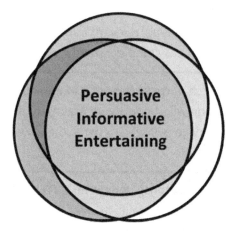

Note that the areas are not all equal. The middle area that overlaps all three speech purposes is by far the biggest. When it comes to speech purpose, we don't want a piece of the PIE. We want all of it!

Sometimes, we talk about speaking being inspirational or motivational. I'm not sure these are useful distinctions to the PIE purposes. Perhaps it is most helpful to think of inspirational or motivational speaking as being a subset of persuasive speaking that requires an audience to take action. As will be evident from the discussion above, if you wish to persuade an audience to take action, you will be more successful by including all the speech purposes.

3.2 Speech Topic – What Are You Speaking About?

The next step is to work out what you will speak about. The amount of freedom you have to decide what you speak about will depend on your specific situation. If you have been told by your boss at work what to present, you have a lot less freedom than someone choosing to give a speech at a Toastmasters club.

Topic Ideas

When it comes to selecting a topic, first you must make sure that any topic fulfills any specific requirements or instructions you have been given. These might be directions from your boss or an event planner or requirements for a certain type of speech such as a TED talk or Toastmasters contest speech. Whatever these are, your speech MUST fulfill these requirements or else you will annoy the person who asked you to speak. Worse still, you may even be ineligible for the event you are trying to speak at.

After meeting the specific requirements, the topic remains a choice for you after considering two important factors:

1. What are you passionate about?
2. What does the audience want?

If you are not passionate about your speech topic then you are making your job much harder. We saw in Chapter 2 that passion is an important tool for boosting your confidence and making you more engaging to your audience. If your speech bores you then you can absolutely guarantee it will bore your audience!

You might not be passionate about your general topic because, for example, you have to talk about an area of your work that does not captivate you. Nevertheless, you can still inject your own areas of experience, interest, stories, and humor within that general topic to increase your enthusiasm. Also remember that in the context stage of your speech preparation, you resolved the question, "Why are you speaking?" You can add to that, "Why does your speech topic matter?" The more important the information you have to share, the more necessary it is that you share it.

Unfortunately, passion is not enough. I could speak forever about chess but most people would not want to hear it. The other factor you must consider is what the audience wants. In some instances, you might be thinking your speech should be more about what your audience needs than wants (such as a staff training or continuing professional development program). You will struggle to have as much of an impact if you just hit them over the head with this: "You need this so you better listen to me!" You will be more effective by showing the benefits to them of what they need so that it should be something they want too. Your responsibility as a speaker is to make sure that when you have finished speaking, you have left them with something valuable.

When you have met the specific requirements, and identified what you are passionate about and what your audience wants, you have found your topic sweet spot.

The Topic Sweet Spot

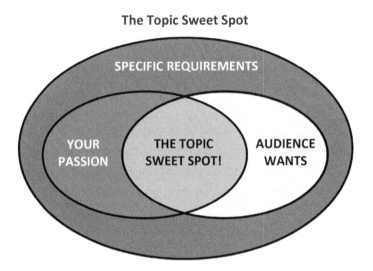

Message Ideas

Once you know what your topic is, it's time to get more specific and work out what the overall message of your speech will be. It might never have occurred to you before that every speech should have a message. A message in a speech is important because:

- it gives your speech purpose and meaning
- it helps organize your speech and give it direction (as we will see in the structure section)
- it gives the audience a clear, valuable benefit from listening to you.

The Message Funnel

The Message Funnel works in two stages and is designed to help you create content for your speech and then refine it down to a key message.

As you sit down to create your speech, you might find yourself in one of two very different situations. You might have a blank sheet of paper in front of you and be creating your speech from scratch. Or you might have detailed facts, reports, notes, and information that you are expected to use as the basis for your speech.

For both of these circumstances, you can use the Message Funnel tool, though you will use it slightly differently in each instance. In the blank paper scenario, you are using the Message Funnel primarily to generate ideas and stories leading to an overall message. In the second scenario, you are using the Message Funnel primarily to filter the information you have down to an overall message.

The Message Funnel

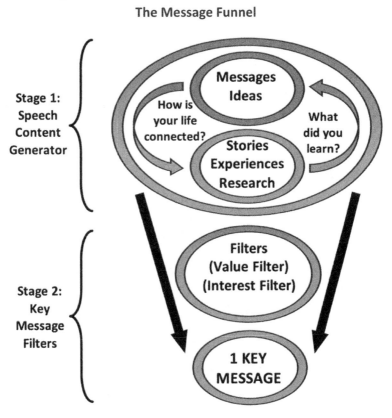

Stage 1: Speech Content Generator

The top of the Message Funnel is a cycle so you can start at any point and continue around until you have generated enough content to use.

1. If you know what you want to speak about, you can think about the possible ideas and messages you could use.
2. To bring these to life, ask yourself how your life or work is connected to these ideas and messages.
3. This should lead you to stories, experiences, or research that you can share. You can also start at this point when you know that you want to speak about a specific story or experience but you are not yet sure what the underlying message of your speech is.
4. After identifying stories, experiences, or research, ask yourself what you learned from them. This should lead you to ideas and messages and back to 1 above, where you can continue around the cycle for as long as necessary.

If you started with a blank sheet, you might need to go around the Stage 1 cycle a few times to gain enough content to work with. If you started with a lot of ideas and information to share then you will use the Stage 1 cycle more to see how they connect to each other.

Stage 2: Key Message Filters

Stage 1 should have generated lots of content you can use for a speech. Most speeches will benefit from having just one key message and for that, you can use the Key Message Filters. The reason why having one key message is important is that more than one message may be confusing for an audience to follow or remember. You can share more than one idea with your audience but they should clearly be linked to the overall message. What you should avoid at all costs is a long list of different ideas, messages, or stories that are seemingly unconnected to each other.

There are two Key Message Filters you can use, but first, here's an important warning:

WARNING ABOUT USING THE KEY MESSAGE FILTERS:

Don't let these filters block you from generating speech material or hold you up if you have little time to prepare. If you strive for perfection, you might decide that your material is never good enough. If you find them helpful, use these filters to sift out the best material from what you have and to make your speech better.

The Value Filter

The best service you can provide to your audience is to give them value. There is a simple formula we can use to show this:

$$\text{Value} \quad = \quad \frac{\text{Importance x Relevance}}{\text{Ability to Implement}}$$

In other words, the value of a speech to an audience is increased by how important and relevant to them it is. The value is decreased by how hard the advice from the speech is to implement.

Three Value Filter examples:

Important but not relevant

Learning how to survive in the desert without food is important but might not be relevant if the audience will not find themselves in that situation. (Note: It could be made relevant if the purpose of the speech was not to share how to survive such a situation, but rather to entertain the audience by sharing such experiences and perhaps share other wisdom that is more applicable to them such as how to be resilient when you have given up hope.)

Relevant but not important

Learning how to buy groceries is relevant to most people but not important as most people know how to do this.

It is still possible to have a good talk based on something that is not very important if the message is nevertheless highly relevant and easy to implement. One of my favorite TEDx talks is "How to use one paper towel" by Joe Smith. Though less than five minutes long, this talk forever changed how I dry my hands!

Important and relevant

Learning how to become a millionaire might be both important and relevant to most people because it could change their lives for the better by providing them with financial security. The value would be determined by how easy or hard it was to implement. If the audience member requires $900,000 to invest then it is probably impossible for them and therefore the talk is of little value. By contrast, if the audience member only needs $100, then the talk may be of great value. (Of course, anyone promising you can make $1 million from $100 is probably selling a scam!)

Because value is audience-focused you can see how the same speech will be of different value to different audiences, so this is another reason why you should always be focused on who your audience is.

The Interest Filter

The Interest Filter is a simple filter to work out if your audience will be interested in what you have to say. It is very unlikely that you will find yourself presenting a completely original message that has never been heard before. If you are, you are lucky!

More likely, your message will be something that the audience has a degree of familiarity with. If you want to hold their interest, then the less original the message is, the more original your stories, experiences, and delivery must be.

The true crime of speaking is to tell the audience something they already know using examples they already know. This is boring! At the other end of the spectrum, if you are fortunate enough to be sharing an original message in an original way then you are a speaking god!

All that really matters though is that you are on the "interesting" side of the line in the following diagram.

The Interest Filter

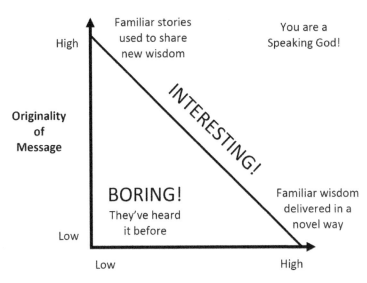

Originality of Stories, Experiences & Delivery

Original Messages

Finding a truly original message is not only hard but if you manage it, you may face another problem. The audience may not be ready for it and you may have a hard time persuading people, depending on how far removed your message is from (their) conventional wisdom. I like to think all messages should on some level be an eternal truth. By eternal truth, I mean something that is widely accepted, common-sense, or at least plausible. That does not mean that the message needs to be obvious, but it should make sense when explained.

Example: Procrastination is good

Consider the argument: "Procrastination is good." Initially, this seems counter-intuitive. Procrastination is the opposite of being efficient and productive which are highly valued skills in most workplaces. However, psychologists conducted an experiment that showed people who put off a task and allowed a problem to incubate were more creative when they returned to the problem. If you believe that creativity is an important skill, you can therefore accept that (at least sometimes) procrastination is good.

As you can see from the Interest Filter diagram, the less original the message is, the more original your stories or overall presentation need to be.

Original Stories

Throughout history and from the earliest memories of our lives, humans have always loved stories. The best stories or experiences to tell are the ones that are personal to you. The advantage of these is that no one will have heard them before (unless you have previously told them) and so by definition, they will be original. As an added advantage, because they are your stories, you are the expert in them and they will be easier for you to remember when speaking.

To help with looking for original stories, one good idea is to keep a story file. This is simply a collection of stories, events, and experiences that have happened to you. It can take any form such as bullet points, notes, photos, or videos. Any time you see something unusual or remarkable or something funny or embarrassing happens to you, add it to your story file for future use. Toastmasters World Champion Mark Brown recommends searching for stories that "amazed, amused or moved you." A good rule is that if you tell your friends or family about something interesting or funny that happened to you and they receive it well, then an audience may similarly appreciate it.

If your personal story is nevertheless a very familiar experience, you will want to think about how to distinguish it through characters, dialogue, settings, events, and details. More information about storytelling is in Chapter 5.

If you do not have your own story for a particular purpose, your speech can still include someone else's story. The two risks to be aware of here are that the audience may already have heard it and you may not be as vivid in describing it as you would be with your own story. Never make up a story (or facts) that you are trying to pass off as true because, if discovered, you will lose a lot of credibility with your audience.

One Key Message

After you have used the Message Funnel, you should now know what is the one key message for your speech. If you still cannot articulate what it is, then you should use the Message Funnel and Key Message Filters again. **Remember, if you are not absolutely clear on what your key message is then you cannot expect your audience to be clear on it!**

As you move toward structuring your speech, think about what stories, experiences, facts, ideas, and research will support your key message and form the body of your speech. These should not be too difficult to find because you will have considered many of them as you used the Message Funnel to arrive at your key message.

3.3 Speech Maps – How Do You Structure Your Speech?

You are feeling really pleased with yourself. You have a great message to share and a number of stories and pieces of information to illustrate it. At this point in your Presentation Priorities journey, you must avoid both a curse and the biggest mistake that speakers make. To navigate these pitfalls successfully, you need a map. That is what this section will give you.

The Curse of the Script

You might be thinking that it is bad luck when you find out that you have to give a speech (if you don't want to give it). In fact, giving a speech is almost always an opportunity rather than a curse. But, there is an object, commonly used in speaking, that can sometimes inflict a terrible curse on the speaker who gazes

upon it. I'm talking about a script or fully written out speech. If a script is not handled carefully, it can ruin your speech. Here are some of the ways it can curse you if you read it when delivering your presentation:

- Your reading is boring and lacks the normal intonation of conversational speech.
- People stop listening to you because many people switch off when they are read to.
- You lose your place when reading or get the pages out of order. An embarrassing silence follows.
- You misread a word or sentence.
- You hold the physical script up, blocking your face and muffling your voice.

Trying to avoid these pitfalls, maybe you decide to memorize your script. That is when the ultimate curse can strike.

You ... forget ...... your .... speech!

Example: The dangers of memorization

Every year, I like to compete in the Toastmasters International Speech Contest. Contestants have to create and present a speech that is between five and seven minutes. The timing is strict so if you go overtime by more than 30 seconds then you are disqualified. For that

---

reason (among others) it is advisable to have a fully written script so you know exactly how long it will take to deliver. In my first year of competing in 2012, I finished ahead of 30,000 people and came third in the World Championship of Public Speaking.

The following year, I was back, competing in the first round which was a local contest in my home club. I'd taken all the lessons from my previous success and was ready to come back stronger than ever. I stood in front of 12 club members in the basement of an assisted-living facility in Providence, Rhode Island. After just two sentences of my powerful opening, my brain froze. I say "froze" but actually it was very active. It hijacked itself and shut me out from my speech. This internal dialogue then happened:

Me:	"Help! What's next?"
My hijacking brain:	"You'd like to know wouldn't you?"
Me:	"Please tell me!"
My hijacking brain:	"What's it worth?"
Me:	"Anything! Everything!"
My hijacking brain:	"You know by now everyone's noticed you've forgotten your speech don't you?"
Me:	"AAAAAAARRGGGGHHHHHHHHH!"

This was not the first time that my hijacking brain had shut me out from my speech. In such circumstances, it had never, ever, given me the exact words I was trying to remember. Therefore, on that evening in Providence, I didn't waste more than a few seconds before I walked over to my chair and picked up my script to find what I'd forgotten. Because I was so near the beginning, the words I'd forgotten were easy to find. Luckily, I quickly regained my rhythm and was able to complete the rest of the speech successfully (without the script or my hijacking brain).

As I reflected on what went wrong in learning my speech above, I realized that several things had led to me forgetting it:

- I was trying to memorize it word for word rather than just remembering my main points and stories.
- I had been rewriting it up until the evening before. I had not had time to internalize the latest draft of my speech.
- I had not slept much and then had a busy day at work right up to the contest. I simply wasn't prepared to give the speech.

The brilliant Nobel-winning Professor Richard Feynman has a perfectly simple solution to these woes: "Understand, don't memorize."

The Biggest Mistake Speakers Make

One of the main reasons that the curse of the script exists is because of the biggest mistake that speakers make. This mistake takes us back to when we were at school.

Example: A school project presentation

When my daughter Jasmine was in third grade, she had to give a presentation to her class about England, the country where she was born. Though she knew a lot about England and had been there many times, this task was not easy because Jasmine was terrified of public speaking.

"Don't worry Jasmine! Just write out your speech and read it to the class," her teacher said. And once more, the biggest mistake about public speaking was made.

When a teacher tells a student to write a speech and then read it aloud, most students are going to put 99% of their effort into the writing. This is because writing is central to the language curriculum in schools and therefore very familiar to both the teacher and the student. This is in sharp contrast to public speaking, which although it appears in most curriculums, is usually an afterthought. So writing is the comfort zone for teacher and student and then reading it out is an afterthought.

But the mistake gets worse. Remember back to when you were at school. Your writing teacher encouraged you to use unusual, interesting words and to write long, complex sentences. This may be great for literature, but it is (usually) terrible advice for a speech.

The biggest mistake about public speaking is that creating a speech requires writing a work of literature.

This mistake carries on after we have left school. Many people focus more on writing than thinking about what they are actually going to say.

A speech should be more like a conversation.

The similarities and differences between speeches, literature, and conversations are discussed in the next chapter (4.1 Speech Style). Having prepared ourselves against the treacherous curses and pitfalls of speaking, let's now examine what a speech is.

What is a Speech?

A speech is a series of ideas with an overall message.
The message is your destination.
The ideas are your journey.

The importance of the overall message should be obvious by now, given the work done to identify it in the previous section (3.2 Speech Topic). "Ideas" means the actual ideas, stories, and information you will share with your audience. The term includes both original thoughts you have had about your topic as well as the choices you have made when thinking about what additional information to include.

Once we understand a speech as a journey to a destination, we can fundamentally rethink what a speech is. Imagine you were coming on a journey to my house but you don't know where it is. You have a choice of two tools to help you get here: (1) a map or (2) a 400-page novel that lists everything between our two houses. What do you choose?

Imagine if you chose the novel. Here are the directions:

"Take a stroll down your gravel path to your car, enjoying the starlings chirping in the red maple tree. As your car rumbles gently down your driveway, make a right at the end, easing gently past next door's chipped, white fence..."

You'd never get here! The novel is too impractical and cumbersome to use and not helpful. You don't need to know everything between our houses. You just need to know the answers to two key questions. These same questions are fundamental to every speech.

1. **WHERE AM I GOING?**
2. **HOW DO I GET THERE?**

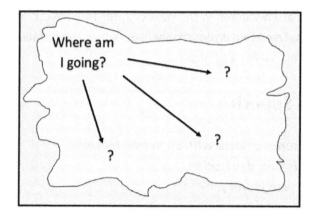

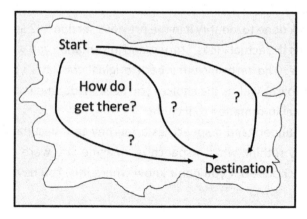

That's why we have maps. Maps show you the essential information. They're easy to understand and remember. When speakers make the biggest mistake of obsessing about the written speech, it's as if they want a speech novel. No wonder it's easy to forget the words. What you need is not a speech novel, but a Speech Map.

What is a Speech Map? A speech map is simply a visual representation of your speech that shows your overall message (your destination) and ideas on the way (your journey).

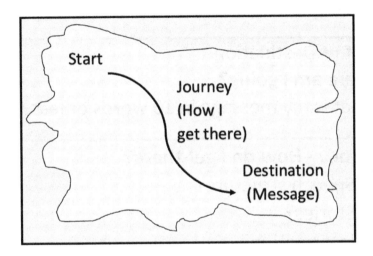

I would strongly argue that **a Speech Map is essential for all speeches**. The beauty of the Speech Map is that it is a win-win for you (the speaker) and your audience. It is easier for you to remember your speech and easier for your audience to understand it. You no longer have to try to hold hundreds of words in your brain in a specific order as if you were in the World Memory Championships!

What Does a Speech Map Look Like?

A Speech Map does not need to look like an actual map although it could do. My daughter Jasmine was able to use a map of famous landmarks to give her presentation about England at school. A Speech Map could use photos or slides. It is most likely to consist of some form of notes or diagrams that are helpful to you. In all that follows it is important to remember that there is no exact and correct way for you to make notes for a Speech Map. What matters is that the notes in your Speech Map are helpful to you.

A simple way to start your Speech Map is to think about the two important questions we have already mentioned as shown in the following diagram.

Start → Destination
Where am I going?
(What is my message in 10 words or less?)

Journey - **How do I get there?**
- Speech structure?
- Stories?
- Information?

The first question ("Where am I going?") is answered by thinking about your overall message. The clearer it is, the better it is and that is why I recommend trying to state your message in ten words or less. This is really important. You may be thinking that your message is more complicated than that or requires a more detailed explanation. The problem is that, by definition, such a message will be harder for you and your audience to remember and understand. Keep reducing your message to its essential elements until you have it down to ten words or less. Often, this will help clarify it to you as well. The beauty of this is that if you were to have a memory lapse when delivering your presentation, this message (your destination) will be easy for you to remember which will make it easier for you to get back on track.

The second question ("How do I get there?") gets you to think about the best route to your destination. There may be many acceptable ways to go. What you need is to choose the one that makes the most sense to you and that you think the audience will understand and appreciate best. As a side note, if you gave the same presentation more than once and got feedback that any part of it was unclear, this is an indication that you need to change the route at that point. This journey part of the speech is where you decide what stories and information to include and what structure you will use for your speech. **As you map out your route remember that everything you include should be helping you explain your message and get to your destination.** This is an editing process. If you have a story or information that you wish to share but it is not related to the message, then you should probably save it for another time.

Creating a Speech Map

When you are creating your Speech Map, there are two very different positions you may be in. You might have a blank sheet of paper in front of you and be starting from scratch or you might already have a fully written speech but realize that you need to turn it into a Speech Map to internalize it for your presentation. Let's look at both methods.

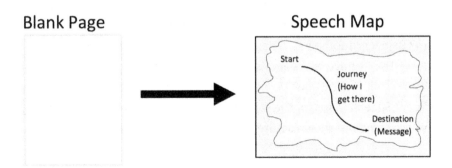

Speech Structures

When starting with a blank page, you should already know your message (see previous sections) but you will need to choose a structure for your speech. Some simple speech structures are:

- **3 Key Points** – Identify the three most important points on the way to explaining your message. Note that three is something of a magic number in speaking. It is a satisfying and easy number to remember. If you have more points to make it will be harder to remember and there is a risk that your speech is becoming a long, potentially boring list of points.
- **Chronological** – List points in time order. This works particularly well when talking about a person's life or looking at events in the past or future.
- **Problem + Solution** – This works well when you are trying to persuade people that you have the answer.
- **Spatial** – This structure focuses on the relationship between people or places. It could be a map but it could also be an organizational chart of people or corporate entities.
- **Demonstration** – This structure helps sell or explain an idea or product. The Speech Map is created by answering the questions: (1) What is it? (2) Why is it needed? (3) What problem does it solve?

You can modify or incorporate these structures together. For example, you can see that the Demonstration speech structure is incorporating both the 3 Key Points and the Problem + Solution structures.

What might these different speech structures look like in Speech Map form? Below are some examples from one of the most famous speeches in history: The "I have a dream" speech given by Martin Luther King Jr. in 1963. You will notice that it is possible to use each structure to create five different Speech Maps for the same speech. Each time, the overall message stays the same but the structure changes how you get there.

3 Key Points

> **Where am I going?** (Message)
> Freedom + justice for black people now
>
> **How do I get there?**
> (3 key points structure)
> - America's broken promise
> - Our suffering
> - The Dream

Chronological

> **Where am I going?** (Message)
> Freedom + justice for black people now
>
> **How do I get there?**
> (Chronological structure)
> - PAST: Slavery
>   Emancipation
>   Suffering
> - NOW: Peaceful protest
> - FUTURE: The Dream

Problem + Solution

> **Where am I going?** (Message)
> Freedom + justice for black people now
>
> **How do I get there?**
> (Problem + Solution structure)
> - PROBLEM: Segregation
>   Inequality
>   Injustice
> - SOLUTION: Peaceful protest
>   Hope + Faith

Spatial

> **Where am I going?** (Message)
> Freedom + justice for black people now
>
> **How do I get there?**
> (Spatial structure)
> - Wash. D.C.:   Emancipation
>   March for Jobs + Freedom
> - USA: Examples of suffering
> - South States: The Dream
> - USA: Freedom

Demonstration

> # Where am I going? (Message)
> Freedom + justice for black people now
>
> # How do I get there?
> (Demonstration structure)
> - **What is it?**   Freedom
>   (or Peaceful Protest)
> - **Why needed?** Examples of suffering
> - **What problem solved?**
>   Injustice + Inequality

Seeing these Speech Maps, you might think that some better represent the actual speech than others. You might also have a strong preference as to which would be most useful for you if you had to give the speech. That's fine. That's the whole point of Speech Maps. You find what works for you. If you needed to add more information, that's also fine. What matters is that this process requires you to visualize your message and how you get to it in your speech. When you have achieved this, you are internalizing your speech which is a very long way from memorizing it.

Full Speech   Speech Map

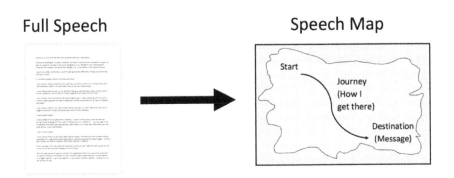

I would certainly recommend using the Speech Map method when creating your speech from scratch. However, there may be any number of reasons why you already have a fully written out speech and you are now wondering how to turn it into a Speech Map. Creating a Speech Map in these circumstances is an exercise in summarizing but, as ever, in a way that makes sense to you.

Print out the speech and draw lines across the page separating each section. A new section occurs any time that the speech moves on to a new point or story. Then label each section so that you can see the journey from start to destination. You now have your Speech Map. Assuming you do not wish to change the speech itself, now you only need to decide how detailed you want your Speech Map to be.

Once again, we can use Martin Luther King Jr.'s "I have a dream" speech. I can't reprint the full text (as it is copyrighted) but it was 1,659 words.

From this, I created notes by splitting the speech into nine sections (see diagram below). This is 66 words but notice that the bold section headings are my own based on what I would do if I had to give this speech. Underneath each section heading are a few brief words that summarize the section. Sometimes these words will be the main idea of the section but they could also be a key phrase or even a transitional phrase that takes you from the previous section into the next section. This Speech Map would work well as a single printed page if you wished to place it on a lectern.

Intro

Slavery
Emancipation Proclamation → now

Our Freedom Check
Constitution = a check
America defaulted

Why Now?
Urgent. Segregation → justice
1963 = beginning. Never rest

Peaceful Protest Together
Discipline not violence. White brothers.

Our Suffering
Police brutality; hotels; etc.

The Dream
"We hold these truths ..."
Brotherhood
Character not skin color

Hope and Faith
Work + struggle together → freedom

Conclusion: Freedom
"Free at last."

But what if this is too much? You can reduce it further to just brief notes. Now we are down to 19 words.

Intro
Slavery
Our Freedom Check

Why Now?
Peaceful Protest Together

Our Suffering
The Dream

Hope and Faith
Conclusion: Freedom

But you could still reduce it more. Here is the Post-it Note version of the speech in just seven words!

Slavery

Freedom Now

Peaceful Protest

Suffering

Dream

I'm a big fan of these types of Speech Maps because you can keep them in your pocket to check over before speaking and for an emergency if you need them when presenting. Because the notes are directional in your journey toward your destination, you only need to glance at them to remember where you are and where you're going.

You might be thinking, "But what if I forget something really important that is not on the note?" Usually, it won't matter because as long as you cover all the points on the Speech Map, you will get your audience to your destination (your message). Of course, if the point you are worried about forgetting is too important to forget, put it on the Speech Map!

The Beginning and the End of Your Speech

The Speech Map will get you through your speech to your destination but there are two very important parts of your speech that you should plan carefully: the introduction and the closing.

The Introduction

A good introduction achieves two crucial objectives.

1. Catch the audience's attention
2. Give them a reason to keep listening

Catch the Audience's Attention

The most important part of an introduction is to catch the audience's attention. If you think about it, this is exactly the same as watching a commercial, movie trailer, tv show, or picking up a book. The first few seconds and minutes will be when most people are deciding whether you are worth listening to or not. This can even happen on a subconscious level. An audience member may wish to listen to you diligently but find their thoughts drifting away if you are boring!

On that basis, try not to focus too much on introducing yourself, thanking the organizers for inviting you, or even telling the audience what you are going to talk about. These are all quite traditional ways to start a speech and risk being boring. While those may all be things you need to share with the audience, either try to keep them very brief or work them in later on.

So, how can you get the audience's attention? Here are six ways:

1. **Story** – A good (personal) story can transport the audience away from just being at a talk. If you do not conclude the story immediately, it is also a way to keep their attention (see below).
2. **Startling Statement** – Say something surprising, controversial, or provocative. The audience may or may not agree with you, but it will wake them up.
3. **Question** – Asking a question causes the audience to reflect upon it. Make sure you give them time to answer in their heads before moving on.
4. **Interesting Statistic/Fact** – As with the startling statement, this should not be obvious. You can combine it with a question ("Did you know …?"). It is usually good to make sense of statistics. If your

statistic was that the world's population grows by 83 million people every year, you could make sense of it by comparing it to adding the population of Germany to the world every year.

5. **Humor (Not a Joke)** – Humor is important in speeches. Humor is seeing the funny side of things and making the audience laugh. The easiest ways to do this are by making fun of yourself or of a common situation that you and the audience are in. Avoid being offensive. Unless you are a comedian, it is very hard to tell jokes that are funny and there is always a risk that they have been heard before.

6. **Captivating Quotation** – Choose something thought-provoking and relevant. Try to avoid overused examples.

Example: Powerful TED talk openings

Here are three examples of powerful introductions from TED talks using a combination of the above techniques:

"Imagine a big explosion as you climb through 3,000 ft. Imagine a plane full of smoke. Imagine an engine going clack, clack, clack, clack, clack, clack, clack. It sounds scary. Well, I had a unique seat that day. I was sitting in 1D." – (using methods 1, 2, 4 above) Ric Elias – "Three things I learned while my plane crashed"

"Sadly, in the next 18 minutes when I do our chat, four Americans that are alive will be dead from the food that they eat." – (2, 4) Jamie Oliver – "Teach every child about food"

"Good morning. How are you? It's been great, hasn't it? I've been blown away by the whole thing. In fact, I'm leaving." – (3, 5) Sir Ken Robinson – "Do schools kill creativity?"

Give Them a Reason to Keep Listening

Having caught the audience's attention, as you start out on your presentation journey, you need to keep their attention. You can do this in various ways:

- **Curiosity** – Tease the audience with something they want to find out. It could be the answer to their problems, how to do something, or even the end of a story. The key is that it is not revealed immediately so the audience needs to keep listening.
- **Value** – Be a gold mine of valuable information, skills, and techniques from the outset. If everything you say from the start is of value, the audience will not want to miss any of it and will want to know more.
- **Entertainment and surprise** – Get the audience to enjoy your presentation from the start. If you can make them laugh, amaze them or surprise them, they will feel good and want to keep listening.

It is not essential in your opening that you tell your audience exactly where you are going in your speech (your message). However, it does not need to be a secret either. The old speech formula of "tell them what you're going to tell them (introduction), tell them (main body of speech), tell them what you told them (closing)" is not at all original, but it can still work if you use the other techniques here to make your speech interesting. The key to knowing when to reveal your message is a balance between the benefits of curiosity (holding it back until later on) and the benefits of letting the audience know where you are going (revealing it sooner). This is a judgment you have to make based on knowing your speech and audience.

The Speech Title

This is a good point to discuss the title of your speech because it has very similar considerations to knowing when to reveal your message. A title may not always be necessary (for example, at a wedding) but in a situation where people are choosing whether to attend your talk, it will help attract audience members. To that end, unless you are so famous that your name is attracting audience members, your speech title should give enough information about your speech without necessarily giving away the point of your speech. If the title reveals the solution to the audience's problem then they may not need to attend your talk! Curiosity and value are helpful here.

Once again, avoid being boring. When *The Office* and *Three Billboards Outside Ebbing, Missouri* first came out and I knew nothing more than their titles, I avoided watching them because I thought they sounded really boring! Years later, I finally saw them and realized my mistake.

The Closing

The closing is important because you have finally arrived at your destination and your message should now be clear and understood by the audience. Here are some important tips to close well:

- **Link back to the beginning** - Audiences love it if there is a chance to link back to the beginning, particularly by finishing a story or anecdote as there is a sense of having come full circle and appreciating how far you have come.
- **Don't rush** – rushing either looks like you are trying to get the speech over with because you don't want to be there or that you have not planned it well.
- **Finish on time** – Organizers and audiences hate it when you finish late. If necessary, adjust your speech in the middle by shortening or leaving parts out so that you arrive at your destination on time.
- **Call to action** – Give the audience something actionable that they can take away and implement immediately. You don't just want the audience to appreciate your speech at that moment. You want to improve their lives.
- **Avoid Q&A** – The energy during Q&A can often fizzle out so it is often better to take questions at some earlier point in your talk and then finish with a strong closing.

How to Use a Speech Map

It should be clear by now that a Speech Map has two primary uses.

(1) You can use it to help **create** your speech.

The map helps you focus on your message (destination) and how to get there. It serves as a filter so that for every story, idea, or piece of information you are considering including in your speech, you should decide whether it helps you get to your destination or not. A Speech Map does not require that you get to your destination in the shortest possible route. It is not saying you can't stop for a moment and acknowledge something interesting or funny (perhaps that connects you with your audience) as you might on a real journey. What the Speech Map filter does however is ensure that you do not go on a wild detour that serves no purpose.

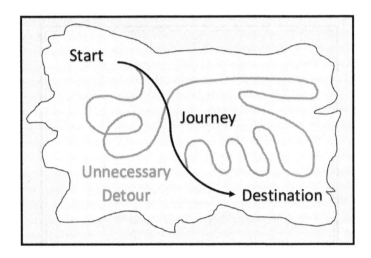

(2) You can use it to help **deliver** your speech.

Your Speech Map can help you deliver your speech because you should start out with a very clear idea of where you are going and how to get there. If you are confident that you can carry the Speech Map in your head then you may not even need notes. Alternatively, you can have anything from the section notes to the Post-it Notes (shown previously) either in front of you or in a pocket for emergencies. Even if you still have a fully written speech with you, I would advise also bringing Speech Map notes as they will always be easier to use than trying to find your place in a script.

If I'm giving a longer speech, I might have my notes somewhere on stage. Occasionally I can walk past them and just check that I'm on course and haven't missed anything. Below is my Speech Map for my one-hour online presentation about Speech Maps (very meta!). These are mini Post-it Notes stuck on a single sheet of paper. Each Post-it Note represents a different section of the presentation. I used pink notes to represent online sections such as activities, games, or slides. Yellow notes represented times when the primary focus was on me speaking. In planning this speech, I was able to move the notes around on this Speech Map until I found the best order. The Speech Map also helped me visualize the spacing in my presentation between my ideas, stories, interactive sections, and online sections.

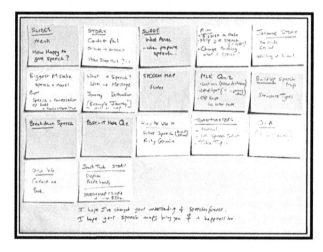

(3) Secret **BONUS** use for Speech Maps!

You don't need to be speaking to use a Speech Map. You can also use them to clarify your thinking on a subject or even to plan a piece of writing. Speech Maps are great tools for clear communication.

What if I Forget Something?

If you forget something when speaking, that is OK. Usually, the audience will never know because they didn't know what you planned to say. Speeches rarely need to be word-perfect and will often sound less authentic if they are too rehearsed. Because you know the direction you are going in, you will get your audience to their destination and will sound more authentic and spontaneous while doing it.

What About Forced Detours?

Sometimes a speech will be interrupted in a way that is unavoidable. It might be a question from the audience, a technical problem, or even a medical emergency. When the interruption is over, it will be your job to continue the journey. In this situation, the Speech Map is much more useful than merely a written speech. You can answer the question (or acknowledge the interruption) and then establish how to get back on track toward your destination. In such circumstances, your spontaneity in handling such a situation will look masterful.

What if I See a Better Route Along the Way?

This is another situation where it is preferable to have a Speech Map. Just as a GPS might recalculate your car journey, you might be in the middle of speaking and realize that there is a better route to your destination. This will benefit everyone because you will also be tailoring your speech to your audience's needs in real-time.

Example: "I have a dream"

Perhaps the most famous example of changing a speech in real-time comes from Martin Luther King Jr.'s "I have a dream" speech. He started his famous speech by reading from his script (though his delivery was still amazing). He was about two-thirds of the way through when his friend, gospel singer Mahalia Jackson, shouted, "Tell

---

'em about the dream Martin!" He brushed aside his written speech and launched into perhaps the most famous speech in history! Now, he didn't completely improvise this. He had used this theme in a speech previously so he knew what he was doing. I would argue that Martin Luther King Jr. had a mental Speech Map in his head and the moment he heard the "dream" suggestion, he realized it was a better route to his destination. In this way, he made history.

Impromptu Speaking

Occasionally you may find yourself in a situation where you have no time to prepare a speech. How do you prepare then? There is a difference between being put on the spot to speak (having no time) and having even a few minutes. If you have a few minutes, your priority is to work out your message as soon as possible. Perhaps you might be thanking or introducing a person at an event. Then, work out the journey. Do you have a story to tell or something funny to say connected to your message? Using these techniques can allow you to sound like you are giving a prepared, well-structured speech even when you were only just asked to speak.

Sometimes you will have no time at all to prepare. An example of this is answering a question in a Q&A session. Another example would be answering a Table Topics question at a Toastmasters meeting where a speaker is called up to answer a question spontaneously. In these situations, you may or may not immediately know where you are going with your speech (or answer). If an idea jumps into your head immediately, you have your destination and then quickly need to choose the best journey toward it. What is the most useful information to share or a good story to illustrate the point? If you do not immediately have an idea, then after a brief pause you need to set off on your speech journey without knowing your destination. Don't panic! In this case, you will head off in what you think is roughly the right direction and start exploring some possibilities. After a bit of time exploring those possibilities, you should decide what your destination is and start heading toward it. This simple process of speaking spontaneously by looking for a destination and heading toward it (putting into practice everything you have learned about Speech Maps) can nevertheless seem like a magical ability to an audience.

Now you know how to use your Speech Map. Speech delivery is discussed more generally in Chapter 4.

3.4 Speech Materials – What Else Do You Need for Your Presentation?

Your speech is nearly ready. While you are still in the content creation stage, there are a few other items you may be creating to help you make your presentation.

Speech Map (and Speech)

The Speech Map section above should have given you all the information you need to know how to map your speech. The exact form that your Speech Map takes (more or less detailed) will be up to you. The most important thing is that it works for you. If you intend to be able to see the Speech Map from where you are speaking, make sure the words are big enough and spaced out enough.

If you also have a fully written speech, you may want this with you too. You can use this before you speak to check specific points or a particular way you worded something. Though I don't generally encourage reading, advice about how to read a speech well is in Chapter 4.

Slides

Slide presentations were once exciting but it has long been known that they hold many pitfalls for speakers. The main piece of advice is **only use slides if they help your presentation**. Examples of how slides can help are by showing pictures, charts, or visuals that clarify a point or show something that is not easily described and understood with words alone. Slides might also help your audience members who identify more as visual learners. If you do not need slides, do not use them. This is exactly the same as thinking about how to get to your destination when creating your Speech Map.

Here are some dos and don'ts for effective slide presentations:

Effective Slide Presentations - Content
Do: <ul><li>Use very few words per slide. Ideally no more than ten. Anything longer should be something you are either capable of saying or it should be a handout.</li><li>Use pictures, video, or media that you couldn't otherwise show. Ideally, use your own material.</li><li>Make the slides clear and easy to read or see. Use a big enough font size and make sure the text contrasts clearly from the background.</li><li>Carefully proof and edit your slides to avoid typos that will look unprofessional and annoy people.</li></ul> **Don't:** <ul><li>Make text heavy slides. If you expect the audience to read them then they won't be listening to you. (If you are reading the slides to them then this is the same problem as reading a speech).</li><li>Use copyrighted images (unless you have permission).</li><li>Have too many slides. Nothing is more depressing than seeing you are on slide 12 of 128.</li><li>Don't get too jazzy with animation, noises, slide effects, and so on as these can be very distracting. Keep your slides simple.</li></ul>

Effective Slide Presentations - Use and delivery

Do:
- Use the slides as part of your Speech Map but you should be adding to what the slide shows or explaining it in your own words.
- Pause to give the audience time to absorb the content of a slide.
- Reveal one point at a time so the audience can focus on it. Many experts believe that the audience should be able to understand a slide within three to five seconds.
- When you have finished with a slide and wish to be the focus of attention again, turn the slides off (or to black) until you are ready for the next slide.
- Make sure you practice using the slides and integrating them with your speech.
- Make sure you can give your speech without slides if necessary (e.g., because of a technical issue).

Don't:
- Don't just rely on the slides to be your speech and read through them, adding nothing else.
- Distract the audience from the slide you are showing by speaking about something else.
- Don't reveal a long list of points as the audience will jump ahead.
- Stand in front of the projector so you are being illuminated and are blocking the slide.
- Use the slides for the first time when you give your presentation.

Handouts

Handouts have some of the same risks as slides in that they can potentially distract your audience. If you are preparing a handout, keep the information on it to a minimum and give the audience time to absorb anything on it that they need to. Consider making it interactive so that key parts are missing that the audience can only fill in by listening to you. Another possibility is to give it out at the end so the audience can take away necessary information without being distracted during your presentation.

Props

Once again following one of our golden rules of public speaking, only use props if they are relevant to helping understand the message and purpose of your speech. If your speech is intended to be entertaining then you might be using a wide array of props. Otherwise, any prop that is just for attention rather than to enhance the message of your speech is really just a gimmick. Similarly, unnecessary props are not helpful. You do not need to use an object as a prop that everybody in the audience is very familiar with. It can be patronizing to use such a prop. As with slides and handouts, remember that props can be distracting if they are not removed from the audience's view at the appropriate time. If you plan on using any props make sure that you practice incorporating them into your speech.

Speaker Introduction

If you are being introduced before speaking then you will want to give a speaker introduction to the person introducing you. Give this to them in advance so that they can familiarize themselves with it. **Make sure that it is short and easy to read.** As with writing a speech, long words and sentences are hard to say and follow. Finally, don't make it boring. As with the opening of your speech, there is a risk of losing your audience here with a boring introduction. Focus less on all your (amazing) achievements and certainly avoid a long list of them. Focus more on what your talk can do for your audience and try to come across as interesting and personable.

CHAPTER 4
COMMUNICATION

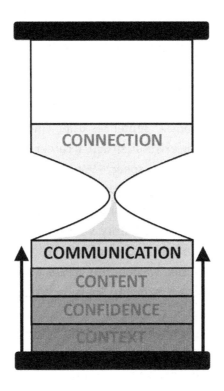

In this chapter…

4.1 Speech Style - How Are You Saying It?

4.2 Practice

4.3 Delivery

Once you know what you are going to say, you must get ready to say it. Practice and delivery have many similarities but you only get one chance to deliver your speech, so practice is very important.

4.1 Speech Style – How Are You Saying It?

You are now a long way into creating your speech. You know why you are speaking, you have your topic and message, and know the points along the way to deliver your message. Next, you need to shift to thinking about the actual words you will use when presenting.

We saw in the previous chapter that the biggest mistake that speakers can make is to think that writing a speech means writing a great work of literature. Partly this comes from our early experience of speaking at school and connecting it to writing at school where teachers encouraged us to write longer, "more complex" sentences using "more interesting" words. In addition, speechwriting exists as an actual career which naturally focuses on the writing part of creating a speech. We have a whole area of language called rhetoric (with lots of unpronounceable ancient Greek terms) which is about effective speaking using compositional techniques. And finally, we have great orators throughout history who famously gave us masterful wisdom through turns of phrase, seemingly designed to be quoted for eternity. No wonder people sit down to create a speech and think they need to conjure up words written like Shakespeare and that must then be delivered like Martin Luther King Jr.!

But for the vast majority of speakers, this is unnecessary. You are not trying to forge wisdom into a mystical text that will be studied and revered for centuries. **When you speak, you are simply speaking to communicate and share your message and ideas.** Guess what? This is what you do every single day of your life.

A speech should be more like a conversation.

Having a conversation is not difficult. Imagine how ridiculous these conversations would be:

Boss: "Hi - can you give me a quick update on our project?"

You: "Can you give me two weeks to think about it, write out some drafts, and script an answer for you?"

Mom: "How was your vacation? What did you do?"
You: "Let me make some notes, research a few quotes and then carefully plan my response to you."

Friend: "Which restaurant shall we go to?"
You: "Give me a week and I'll prepare a slideshow with some possibilities."

In reality, each of these questions should be fairly easy to answer. Or even if there was not a single, simple answer, you would be able to reply in some way that makes sense and gives the questioner some useful information.

A speech is not exactly the same as a conversation. Generally, you will have given it more thought and will use less casual language. There is a spectrum of communication with speeches in the middle of books and conversations.

The Communication Spectrum

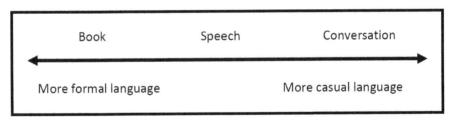

| Book | Speech | Conversation |
| More formal language | | More casual language |

Public speaking borrows some characteristics both from books and conversations, but without understanding the key differences between them, there is a risk of borrowing the wrong characteristics when giving a speech. The table below illustrates how speeches are similar to and different from books and conversations.

Comparing Characteristics of Books, Speech and Conversation

Format

Book: An author's words are written and the reader reads them at the reader's chosen pace.

Speech: One person is speaking to an audience at a pace that must allow the audience to follow along.

Conversation: Two or more people take turns speaking and listening to each other.

Who controls the delivery pace?

Book: Reader (not the author).

Speech: Speaker (not the audience).

Conversation: All people in the conversation (by taking turns, interrupting, asking questions).

Urgency

Book: No urgency – books take as long as they want to build up to a point.

Speech: Medium urgency – no one will interrupt the speaker but if they waste time they will lose their audience.

Conversation: High urgency – if a speaker does not make their point quickly, someone will usually interrupt them.

Sentence length

Book: Sentences may be long because the reader can go back and reread them.

Speech: Sentences should usually be short because they are easier to say and understand. Usually, the audience only hears a sentence once.

Conversation: Sentences are usually short because they are easier to understand and because it is important to let others speak in a conversation.

Word choice

Book: Often descriptive (for novels) or technical jargon (for non-fiction). Long words can be used in writing because they are easier to read than speak. Readers may look up unknown words in a dictionary.

Speech: Usually very simple. The most important thing is that everyone understands what the speaker says, but there is limited opportunity for the speaker to check this. If using new terms or jargon, the speaker must explain this to the audience. Therefore, it makes sense to err on the side of simplicity.

Conversation: Usually very simple. The most important thing is that everyone understands what the speaker says. If someone doesn't understand they can ask for clarification and the speaker can explain their point again.

Editing and correctness of sentences

Book: The writing is carefully crafted so that it is completely accurate, grammatically correct, and in a logical order.

Speech: The speech should be crafted so that ideas are presented in a logical order. While it is important to use correct language and syntax, there is no single correct way to say it. Only the speaker knows what they plan to say. It is acceptable for the speaker to present ideas in their own words in the moment (and even desirable for it not to sound over-rehearsed).

Conversation: Conversation is spontaneous. Ideas may appear in the random order they are thought of. Grammatical and syntax mistakes are frequently made (e.g., including repetition of words and unfinished sentences).

Slang

Book: Not used unless in dialogue.
Speech: Not used unless in dialogue.
Conversation: Regularly used.

Filler words (um, er)

Book: Not used unless in dialogue.

Speech: Not appropriate unless in dialogue.

Conversation: Regularly used, partly because this gives the speaker thinking time while informing others it's not their turn to speak yet.

Ability to redo

Book: The reader may reread the text as many times as they like.

Speech: Usually, a speaker will only say things once. The most important ideas and the message should be repeated in the speech to make sure the audience definitely hears them.

Conversation: A person can always ask a speaker to clarify or repeat something they said if they do not hear it or understand it.

Ability to reflect

Book: The reader may take as much time as they like to reflect on the text.

Speech: There will be time to reflect after the speech. If a speaker wants the audience to reflect during the speech then they must pause and give the audience time to reflect.

Conversation: There is usually little time to reflect as conversations are spontaneous and fast-paced.

The Value of Simplicity

In my years of practice and experience as a lawyer and teacher in the UK and the US, I noticed something that troubled me. Whenever I saw a lawyer or teacher give a presentation to their peers, they typically filled their speeches with convoluted ideas and technical jargon. Even as a fellow professional, these presentations were often hard to follow. Then I realized something. Most of these speakers were nervous (on some level) about speaking to their peers and so they were using their language as a shield. Their reasoning seemed to be that "the more complicated I can make this sound, the harder it will be for people to follow me and the more of an expert they will think I am."

It is certainly useful to feel like an expert. It can justify those years devoted to college qualifications or those high lawyers' fees! But I believe this reasoning is all wrong.

A true expert is one who can explain complicated ideas and make them sound so simple that everyone can understand them.

Such skill cannot easily be copied, so professionals (and speakers) should not worry that speaking in simple terms means everyone will be able to do what they do. And as we know by now, the audience will certainly appreciate being able to understand what they are listening to.

The other possibility when speakers use jargon and complicated terms is that they are struggling to make sense of the subject and are just copying something they have read or heard. As Professor Richard Feynman said, "If you cannot explain something in simple terms, you don't understand it." In such circumstances, a speaker should keep trying to make sense of the materials they wish to present and only use their own words to explain them. In any case, creating the Speech Map, as described in the previous section, should help with this as it forces the speaker to understand what they are talking about.

4.2 Practice

A Warning About Harmful Practice

"Practice, practice, practice!" is advice you will often hear about mastering any skill. I don't completely agree. Practice is very important but, in the case of public speaking, you must remember why you are practicing. You are practicing so that you can deliver your speech as well as possible. Any practice which is not helping you achieve that may be harmful.

Two examples of harmful practice:

(1) You have been dramatically changing your speech so that you have not internalized the new version. A colleague offers you a chance to practice it in front of them. You get confused by the old and new versions of your speech and deliver the practice speech badly. As a result, this damages your confidence and makes you doubt your ability to give the speech successfully. It would have been better to turn down the opportunity to practice publicly until you knew your speech better.

(2) You never turn down a chance to practice your speech and as a result, you have given it three times a day in front of different people for over a week. As a result, you are getting bored with your speech and just find yourself going through the motions now. Remember from Chapter 2 (Confidence) that you need energy to give your speech. Too much practice can result in sliding toward the apathy end of the Speaker Nerves Spectrum. When you deliver it, you want it to be fresh and exciting.

Note that in both of the above examples, there may be people who wouldn't suffer the consequences mentioned. If you can mess up a practice and it doesn't affect your confidence or you can practice endlessly without losing your enthusiasm, you might continue to do such practices. I believe that speech practice is such a personal skill, that you cannot just be told by other people how you should do it. The key is to know yourself and what will help you the most.

A Warning About Not Practicing

However, please don't think that the above warning gives you permission not to practice! Even if you are talented and spontaneous enough to perform well when giving a speech for the first time, it will always be better if you have practiced it.

Categories of Practice

What is practice? Practice is the rehearsal of any part of your speech to make it better. Speaking is a whole-body workout and practice is when you are in your speech gym.

There are two main categories of practice. First, you can practice the specific speech that you will be giving. Secondly, you can practice public speaking skills generally. If you have less time to prepare your speech or it is more of a one-off occasion, speech practice will be more useful to you, so we will look at that first.

Speech Practice

When it comes to practicing your speech, you can practice it privately or publicly. Mostly, I prefer private practice for several reasons. I can do it by myself and can do it anywhere. I won't be embarrassed if I make a mistake. If I make a mistake, it's easier to start again or do whatever makes sense next. There are also lots of different ways to practice privately.

Practicing in public (that is, in front of one or more people) can be great experience, especially because it is more like a real presentation in front of an audience. However, it is not always easy to organize. You need to be fairly well prepared before doing this as you do not want to waste your practice audience's time. You also need to know how to deal with any feedback you receive.

Private Speech Practice

There are many different ways to practice privately and many different aspects of your speech to practice. Your preferences and your circumstances may determine which of the following ways you like to practice. I've already likened speech practice to exercise in a gym. While you do not need to do all of the following, the more you can do, the stronger you and your speech will be.

Mental Practice

Mental practice is great because you can do it anywhere, at any time, and usually without anyone knowing. It simply involves thinking your speech through in your head. If I'm lying awake in bed, the night before an important speech, I will practice my speech mentally. It feels like the most useful way to use my time and can help me feel better prepared.

Mental practice can be word specific (as in the actual words you intend to use in the speech) but you can also use it to practice your speech outline. In effect, this is rehearsing the route of your Speech Map (see Chapter 3) so that you know where you are going and how to get there. For example:

First, I'm going to introduce myself with this story ...
Then my first point is ...
To illustrate it, I'll tell this story ...
Next, I'm sharing this data ...
After that, I move on to my second point ...

As you hopefully realize by now, knowing where you are going is far more important than the exact words you're going to use. Another way I practice mentally, especially on the day of a speech, is to use free moments to run through my speech. Right before going on stage, I'm always mentally practicing the first thing I'm going to say.

Read Out Loud - Fully Written Speech

If you have written a speech, reading out loud can be a good way to practice it. Even if you will eventually be delivering the speech without reading it or without notes, the practice of reading it can help you familiarize yourself with it. It is also usually easier to read it from a page than to practice from memory.

I find reading out loud is an easy way to practice early on. When you practice this way, you should read as if you are delivering the speech. This means:

- **Read at the pace you would deliver it.**
- **Pause in appropriate places** (including where you anticipate audience laughter). Use commas or ellipses (...) to show this in the written speech.
- **Emphasize the same words** you would when speaking on stage (and emphasize them in the script using bold, underline, or a bigger font).

It can be helpful to print your speech so that you only have one sentence on a line. You also might want double spacing between the lines. That way it is easier to read.

If you read your speech in the same way you will eventually deliver it then you can also check the timing of it. It may be helpful to put times next to each section on your notes. These times can be how long you expect each section to last or what actual time you should be at each section when giving the speech (or both).

If your actual event will involve you reading your speech from paper or on an autocue, then this type of practice is essential and realistic. At the beginning of this chapter we examined the difference between writing for speeches and books. The biggest mistake with a written speech is to make the sentences too long or complicated. Short sentences with language that is easy to understand are important here. Remember, even if you can successfully read out a long sentence, that doesn't mean that the audience will successfully understand it. They only get one go at listening to it. As the speaker, you want to maximize their chance of success.

It is also important that the speech sounds conversational rather than just being read as a narrative. Many people also lose concentration or get bored when they are read to. A conversational speech will help the audience feel more involved and therefore be more interactive for them.

Example: The difference between an author reading and giving a speech

I once attended a performance by author and humorist David Sedaris. He read some passages from his new book to the audience and also shared a commencement address he had recently given. At the end of the evening, he seemed surprised by how well the audience had reacted to his commencement address – it was the highlight of the evening. I think the reason why the commencement address worked better was that it was specifically written to be spoken to an audience, unlike his books.

Read Out Loud - Notes and Bullet Points Speech

If you are practicing from notes or bullet points, you should not be reading out that much. The most important thing here is to make sure that your notes work for you. Factors to consider are:

- **Do you have the correct words written down?** These are either the most important words or topic headings or else words that will trigger your memory to let you know what you are speaking about next.
- **Do you have the fewest words possible written down?** The more words you have written on a page, the harder it will be to find what you want if you need to refer to your notes in your speech.
- **Will you be able to read your notes?** Are the words big enough that you will be able to read (or see) them from where you are

speaking? Ideally, you don't want it to be obvious that you are referring to notes.

As you practice you can refine this. You can start with more notes and gradually reduce them as you become more familiar with your speech. As a rule, I try to use not more than a Post-it Note for a short speech and one page for a longer speech such as a one-hour keynote.

Modular Practice

Modular practice is one of my favorite ways to practice. It involves breaking your speech into sections which should be easy as you will know these sections from having planned your Speech Map (see Chapter 3). Each section represents a new point or story in your speech. Instead of practicing from start to finish conventionally, you can now practice any section of your speech and also focus on how to transition from one section to the next.

Before I used modular practice, typically what happened when I practiced was this: I would start at the beginning, make a mistake, stop, and start all over from the beginning again. Guess which part of my speech was the most rehearsed? Naturally, it was the beginning. The problem I had was that I was never getting to practice the ending. To compensate for that, I can now use modular practice to practice my speech in reverse. Imagine my speech has seven sections. I'll practice the ending (section seven). Then I'll practice section six leading into seven. Then I'll practice sections five, six, and seven, and so on until I'm doing the whole speech.

Floor Modular Practice (Stage Mapping)

If you have a big stage for your speech and are going to move about, you can practice your stage movement through modular practice as well. This is similar to the practice of "blocking" used to place actors in precise places on stage (in a play) or set (in a movie). In your speech, you can plan to speak in a different place on stage for each section or story. When I practice, I put a numbered sheet of paper on the floor for each section. The paper also has one or two keywords on it to tell me what that section is and sometimes an arrow to show me the direction I move in next. I then practice the speech standing at each sheet of paper. This allows me to practice my movement on stage and transitions between sections as well as my actual speech. It is easy to adjust the location of different sections (by moving the sheets of paper on the floor) so that they work well together. Even if you are practicing in a smaller area than your actual stage, you are still learning the relative positions where you will deliver each part of your speech and the directions you have to move between them.

As you do more of this, you start to build muscle memory of your speech. While you move around the stage your body and mind work together to remember what comes next in your speech. This can be helpful even if you are unable to move much during the actual delivery of your speech (for example if you were giving a TED talk and had to stay on the red dot). When I've practiced a speech with movement but then given it from one position (even sitting down), I find that my brain is still mentally moving around the stage and helping me remember my speech!

Example: Stage mapping my speech, "The Bear Necessities"

Below is the stage mapping of my speech, "The Bear Necessities." Each number is a different section of the speech and would be represented by a separate sheet of paper on my floor when practicing. You can see that I managed to use almost all of the stage.

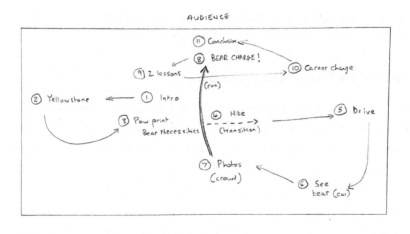

Timing Practice

Nothing is more depressing than a speaker with 100 slides left to show when their allotted time for speaking is up. The timing of your speech is always important. Neither the person who asked you to speak nor the audience wants you to go overtime. It is always better to finish a few minutes early rather than a few minutes late. Therefore, one aspect of your practice must be to ensure that your speech is the correct length to fill the time available but also not be too long.

When practicing, you must try to speak at a normal speech pace so that the timing is realistic. Try not to skim through the words faster than you will be saying them on stage. When delivering your speech, be careful not to let any nervous energy make you rush through your speech faster than you practiced.

To help you with timing, it is useful to build flexibility into your speech. Flexibility can help you speed up or slow down when speaking. It also allows you to adjust the overall length of your speech. If you were asked to speak for one hour but at the last minute you find out you only have 45 minutes to speak, you need to have the flexibility to know how to adjust your speech. This means that you should decide which sections, stories, or points of your speech to leave out. You certainly do not want to just try speaking more quickly as you will be harder to follow and your speech will have less impact.

Two pieces of information are necessary to know how to adjust your speech in this manner. First, you must know (from practice) how long each section is. This means that if you are asked to cut 15 minutes of speaking time, you can easily take out 15 minutes of material from your speech. Not all sections are created equal, so the second thing you must know is how important all the different sections are. You will (usually) want to remove the least important part of your speech. The Speech Map (see Chapter 3) is helpful here. Your overall destination is the same, but your journey there has become shorter. You must make sure that your shorter version of the speech still gets you to where you need to go.

I recommend thinking about your speech as having waypoints in it. Just as you use a Speech Map to show you where your speech is going, each of the main points or sections that get you to your destination becomes a waypoint. It is worth calculating in advance at what time you should be at each waypoint in your speech. Then, by checking where you are in your speech against the time, you can see whether you need to speed up or slow down. This might also determine whether you have more or less time to give extra examples or take questions as you are progressing.

All over the world, Toastmasters are familiar with a system of green, yellow and red cards or lights shown to them by a person timing them when speaking. Green represents the minimum required speaking time and red represents the maximum. Yellow is the midpoint between the two. You can find apps online that copy this system if that would be helpful for practice.

Audio Practice

Audio practice is worth doing if you want or need to hear what you sound like. This might either be because you are trying a particular microphone in a particular place or if you want to check your voice generally. If you are soft-spoken, you may think that you are really projecting your voice, but an audio recording may reveal that you still need to project it more. An audio recording can also be useful to check your vocal variety throughout the speech. Is it too loud or soft for too long? Can the quieter bits still be heard?

Audio recordings are ideal to listen to when commuting, in a gym, or anywhere else you might listen to music or podcasts. This will help internalize your message. In a car, you can then also practice saying your speech while driving (as long as you keep focused on the road too!).

Video Practice

Video practice can also include audio practice. It is a particularly effective way to check your body language and facial expressions. Do you have any distracting habits which should be controlled or eliminated? Examples of this might be pacing backward and forward on the stage (rather than moving with purpose) or any repetitive gesture. When watching video, it is very easy to focus on what is being said, so you might want to try switching the volume off and just watching the video silently. Then you can truly assess how effective your body language is. If you are practicing for an online speech, use the video to make sure that your lighting is good and your camera frames you well so that you will be clearly seen at all times.

Technology Practice

Technology is everywhere in speaking now – microphones, speakers, recorders, cameras, computers, lighting, slideshows, smartphones, online meeting rooms, and so on. Everything that is technological has a chance to go wrong! It makes sense to practice using as many of these as possible so that when it comes to the actual event you can focus on your speaking. It is also a good idea to have a contingency plan for technology failure. For example, if your slides don't work, can you still give your speech?

Slides Are Not the Presenter!

We have already discussed how to create and use presentation slides in Chapter 3. Below are some further tips to make sure you control your slides and not the other way around:

- **Don't just read the slide**. If there are words to be read, let the audience do that. Your job is to introduce, describe, elaborate, explain, analyze, synthesize or evaluate what is on the slide. If you are merely repeating the slide then you are not needed!
- **Don't hide behind the slides**. "Basically, this slide is pretty self-explanatory." Instead of reading, some presenters prefer to say (basically!) nothing. Try to find the middle ground of adding value to each slide without patronizing the audience by telling them what they can see for themselves.
- **Don't use the slides as a crutch**. Ideally, you should be able to give your presentation without needing slides. Otherwise, you are relying on technology working to be able to give your presentation. Using the slides as a prompt is OK as long as you then add value to them. It would also be sensible to have a hard copy of notes or slides in case the technology fails.

All of the above problems tend to occur when speakers are afraid that they don't know their talk and want the slides to do the presentation for them. If you have used the Speech Map process from Chapter 3 and the confidence tips from Chapter 2, you should not be in this position. You know what your message is and how to get there. You know that this talk is focused on your audience, not you.

- **Don't compete with the slide**. A lot of speakers put up a new slide with words or information for the audience to absorb and then speak at the same time! As an audience member (who is a visual learner), I always focus on the slide and ignore the presenter. It should always be clear where the audience's attention should be focused. If it is the slides, give the audience time to look at them. If it is you, call attention back to yourself and consider turning off the slideshow or going to a black screen so that the audience can give you their attention.
- **Don't stand in front of the slide**. Nothing is more distracting than a blinded speaker who has half of their slide projected onto their clothes and face. Work out where you need to stand so that you can speak without getting in the way of the slide.

Prop Practice

A prop is something physical that you are using or showing in your speech to improve it. It could be a product, a picture, a piece of clothing, or any other type of object. Your prop shouldn't be just a gimmick. A prop is used to enhance a speech whereas a gimmick is something designed to attract attention but of little relevance to the speech.

You will want to practice using the prop so that you can smoothly transition into and out of showing it. You don't want the prop to be a distraction before or after you use it, so think about where it will be kept during your speech. Avoid using props that are obviously just for the sake of having a prop as this can be annoying. Examples would be showing a simple object that everyone already knows what it is and can picture in their heads without seeing it on stage.

There are famous examples of props being used well. Steve Jobs used the iPhone as a prop in his great speech introducing the new product. Bill Gates used mosquitoes in his TED talk about malaria. (In some way, these became a distraction to his audience but that was his point. He wanted the audience to be bothered by them and bothered about malaria.)

Public Speech Practice

Practicing in front of other people requires more organization than practicing by yourself. The main difference between a public speech practice and delivering your speech at the actual event is that the focus in practice should be on you the speaker (rather than the audience). That doesn't mean ignoring all the tips from Chapter 2 (Confidence) about focusing on the audience. It just means that the primary purpose of the practice should be to help you get better for your main event. If the practice is not helping you then you should not be doing it. Questions to consider here are:

- Why am I doing this? (What do I hope to get out of this practice?)
- What am I mainly focusing on in this practice?
- How will I evaluate this practice? (Audience feedback, video, self-reflection, etc.)
- Who is my practice audience? (Who is available and useful to you?)
- What do I want my practice audience to focus on in my speech?
- How will I use my audience feedback? (See Feedback below.)

I have two general rules that work for me when selecting a practice audience. I try to avoid using people who will be in the audience for the real event. If my speech or humor involves surprise, I prefer people not to have previously seen it. Also, I tend to avoid practicing in front of my family. I just find it is easier to take feedback from strangers, friends, or acquaintances. Family can find it harder to give honest feedback and I feel more self-conscious in front of them!

Feedback

Quality feedback is like gold dust. But how do you know what quality feedback is? By now, you should not be surprised to know that quality feedback is anything that will make your speech better. Here is what you need to know about feedback.

- **Feedback must work for you** – I think the first rule of feedback is that you have to know what to accept and what not to accept. You can only say things in your speech if they work for you. It's your speech and nobody else's. In the same way, when I coach speakers, I sometimes comment that I might say or do a specific thing if it were my speech, but because it's their speech, they need to decide if that works for them.
- **Be your own evaluator** – You should continually be evaluating your speech. As the person who is thinking about it the most, that makes you the expert on it and therefore in the best position to know what to change.
- **Three simple evaluation questions** –
    - What was the message of the speech?
    - What worked well in the speech? [What did you like?]
    - What could be improved in the speech? [What didn't you like?]

  You can give these questions to a practice audience. The first question is important because your message should be very clear. If they are still not getting it, you need to make it even clearer!
- **What to do with suggestions for changing your speech** – After you have practiced your speech, you will have got feedback from your audience and also will have your own opinions. How do you decide what you will do to your speech next?

To change or not to change?

You + audience want change

This is easy and should be your top priority. You probably already sensed something in your speech wasn't quite working and now the audience has given you that feedback too. Change it!

You want change + audience doesn't want change

This is your second priority. If you feel that there is something in your speech that needs to be changed then change it! It is worth trying to understand why the audience doesn't want it changed. Did they notice it and like it as it is? Were they not aware of it?

You don't want change + audience does want change

This is the hardest decision because you and your audience disagree about what to do and they want you to change a part of your speech. Why do they want the change? Is it unclear? Do they not like it? Do they not understand it? Why do you want to keep it? Is it central to your message or have you just grown fond of it? Would this part work better if you changed another part of your speech or made your overall speech clearer? Can you test it with another audience and see if you get the same reaction? You will also want to ask these questions where different members of the audience disagree and make conflicting suggestions about whether you should make a change or not.

You + audience don't want change

Generally speaking, you can keep this part of your speech the same. Always be prepared to change it in the future if necessary.

- **Don't change your speech too much** – Your speech should always be your speech. Remember that you have carefully created a key message and journey with your Speech Map from Chapter 3. You are in charge of the map and have the best overview of where you are going, so make sure you do not keep changing your speech at the suggestion of others in such a way that you end up making a detour and getting lost on the way to your destination. As you make changes, they should be clarifying and helping your speech.

- **Return to your best evaluators** – If you find a person that consistently gives you good feedback, keep returning to them. Lynn Potter is a Toastmaster in Rhode Island who always enlightens me with invaluable insight about my speeches. Thank you, Lynn!

Speaking in Public When Not Practicing a Speech

I am a big believer in the idea that any time you speak in front of other people, you are practicing public speaking. This could be asking questions in a meeting, speaking to customers at work, an interview, and so on. Speaking with confidence and clarity in these situations helps improve your public speaking, so take the opportunity to speak as well as you can. If I'm sitting in a meeting and know I'm going to ask a question, I start mentally practicing it so I know it will be as clear as possible when I say it.

Public Speaking Skills Practice

So far, everything in this book has focused on you working toward giving a specific speech. If you have more time until your speech, or public speaking is something that you are going to do on multiple occasions then it is worth taking time to practice the basic skills required. People in this situation often join Toastmasters because it is the perfect venue to practice public speaking over a longer period. Toastmasters focuses a lot more on speaking skills than the actual content of your speech.

Focus on One Skill at a Time

Each public speaking skill that is new to you will take time to get used to. I recommend that each time you speak or practice, only focus on one skill.

Example: Trying to practice too much at once

Many years ago, when I was a trainee lawyer, I took part in an advocacy training program. I gave a short speech and a judge who was coaching me told me three things to improve. As I gave my speech again, I failed at all three! It felt like juggling plates and I couldn't keep everything in my head at the same time. A senior advocacy instructor then told the judge that he should have given me just one skill to work on. I tried again focusing on just one skill and this time I was successful.

The Basic Public Speaking Skills

The diagram below shows the basic public speaking skills that any good speaker needs.

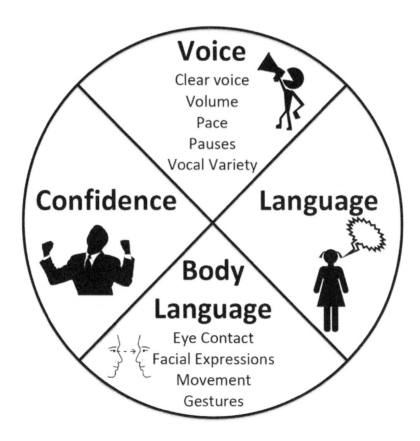

Voice

Using your voice is the most important basic skill because, without your voice, you have no speech!

Clear Voice

You must pronounce your words as clearly as possible to maximize the chance of your audience understanding every word. We've all had the experience of discovering that actual song lyrics are different from what we thought an artist was singing. That matters less because the primary aim of a song is our musical enjoyment. Speakers do not have the same luxury. If you have an accent that the audience may not be used to, it is essential to give them time to "tune in" to how you speak. In America, I always start my first couple of sentences carefully because my American audience may not be expecting a British accent!

Volume

What is the point of speaking if the audience cannot hear you?! This is the most frustrating situation for an audience and one that I notice at a lot of school events where kids are asked to speak but are not given any opportunity to practice. The act of speaking requires projecting your voice. It is not OK to speak and hope that everyone can hear you. You need to guarantee that they can. To find the right level of projection, I imagine that my voice has a volume control from zero to ten (zero = silent, ten = screaming). If five is my normal speaking voice, then when I am public speaking I want to be one or two levels higher (that is, a six or seven) to make sure I'm projecting. Another way of thinking about this is that I'm speaking slightly louder than my normal, comfortable voice. If there is a microphone you should be speaking close enough to it that it amplifies your voice and adjust your distance from it so that the audience can easily hear you.

Pace

Pace is a lot like Goldilocks' search in the three bears' house – you want to find the pace that is just right. The biggest mistake that speakers make here (especially nervous ones) is they speak too quickly. Usually, this is because they want the whole experience to be over as soon as possible so they are trying to rush through. Do not do this! It makes your speech harder to follow, it makes you look less confident and it makes your message look less important. The other situation where speakers speak too quickly is where they have too much information to share in too little time. In this situation, you should use the Speech Map (from Chapter 3) to work out what is essential and cut out information that is not necessary.

At the other end of the spectrum, some speakers can speak too slowly. Imagine a teacher or professor droning on in class. This will be boring so it is important to speed up a little and add some energy.

Your pace may need to change with your audience. This could be based on where the audience is from. For example, I've noticed that Americans from New England often speak faster than Americans from other areas of the country, so they may want you to speak a bit faster too. Other factors to consider are the circumstances around when you are speaking. If you are speaking immediately after your audience has had lunch they may be a bit lethargic and you may need to inject a little pace and energy to wake them up.

The final point to note about pace is that whatever your "just right" pace is, it should not always stay the same but you should vary it as appropriate. This is discussed more in vocal variety below.

Pauses

Pauses are a very important part of speaking. They emphasize points. They give the audience time to reflect or answer a question in their heads. They can add drama and tension to a speech or story. They also ensure that the speaker maintains a good pace without rushing into the next sentence.

Probably the hardest thing for speakers to understand about pauses is that a pause on stage feels infinitely longer to the speaker than it actually is for the audience. A common fear that speakers have is that they must fill all silence but that is not true. It is far better to take a silent moment to consider your next point than to fill it with noise (see the section on avoiding filler words in Language below). If you want to pause for a certain number of seconds, you can try counting as follows: "One – thousand – two – thousand – three – thousand" for three seconds. Another good rule is that when asking a (rhetorical) question, pause for long enough so that the audience members can answer it in their heads. One way to know how long this should be is for you also to answer the question in your head.

Vocal Variety

If you think about any story, movie, book, or piece of music, you will realize that they all have lots of ups and downs. Variety and contrast are important to keep the reader's or viewer's or listener's attention. A story that proceeds at the same, predictable pace with no variety quickly becomes very boring.

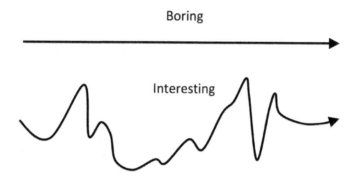

The same is true for speaking! No matter what your natural style of speaking is, you will need to vary it to maintain interest among the audience. There are three easy ways to do this:

- **Volume.** Above, I mentioned projecting your voice so that your normal public speaking voice might be a six or seven out of ten. Don't keep it static here though. Look for moments when you can be louder or quieter. Here are some examples:

Be louder when …	Be quieter when …
<ul><li>Excited</li><li>Angry</li><li>Surprised</li><li>Frustrated</li><li>Beginning your speech</li><li>Ending your speech</li><li>You need more energy in the room</li></ul>	<ul><li>Sad</li><li>Thoughtful</li><li>Confused</li><li>Bored</li><li>When you want the audience to think</li><li>You need more calm in the room</li></ul>

Note that the emotions referred to could be your state of mind as you are telling a story or making a point, or they could be a character's dialogue that you are saying. Also, no matter how quietly you speak, you must still be audible to the audience or else there is no point saying it. Remember too, that on the quieter side, you might sometimes convey information by saying nothing and showing a simple expression (see Body Language below).

- **Pace**. To some extent, changing the speed you talk at may reflect your change in volume too. The emotions that require you to talk more loudly may also benefit from talking more quickly and the quieter emotions may match slowing down your pace. You may also want to slow down for important parts of your presentation. Be careful though. Talking fast for too long will be hard to follow. Talking slowly for too long will be boring.

- **Emotion**. It is good to change emotions during your speech so that the audience members connect with you and stay focused on you. This does not require taking them through an emotional roller-coaster but rather looking for opportunities to incorporate feelings that are different from the majority of your talk.

Warming Up

As a speaker, you want to look after your voice. There are many exercises that actors and singers recommend to warm up their voices. One of my favorites is to hum. One reason is that it is a gentle exercise for the throat. Another is that you can do it very quietly, so you can warm up even while in a room full of people.

Confidence

Confidence is such an important part of basic speaking skills that we have already devoted a whole chapter to it (see Chapter 2). The reason that this appeared earlier in the book is that your confidence is something you need to work on and control from the moment you know you will be speaking.

On stage, the appearance of a speaker being confident is necessary for the audience to be comfortable and then able to focus on the message. If this is difficult for you, look back at the faking it till you make it section of Chapter 2. Like the captain of a plane, remember to put your audience at ease and don't forget to smile!

Language

The skill of practicing good language when speaking is not so much about using the soaring rhetoric of a Kennedy, Churchill, or Lincoln. Rather it is about controlling the words that come out of your mouth so that the audience can easily understand you and does not get annoyed. Here are the three main areas to work on.

Clear Language

It is very important that the language that you use is clear and can be easily spoken (by you) and understood (by the audience). If you cannot say the words or sentences easily in practice, simplify them. A true expert can explain a complicated idea in the simplest terms and that is what you should aim for. Can a school kid or a non-expert understand you? Where possible, try to avoid using technical jargon or acronyms. If you have to use them, at least make sure that you explain them and that the audience understands them. A final consideration is whether any foreign, cultural, or generational language will be understood by your audience.

Example: A British speaker in America

I will typically eliminate British terms when speaking to an American audience unless I think they are well understood in the USA. Always keep an eye on your audience when speaking to make sure they understand you. Even after 15 years of living in America, I'll occasionally say something and realize from the blank expressions of my American audience (or my American family!) that I must have just used a British word or phrase that needs explaining.

Appropriate Language

In a nutshell, avoid swearing, offensive words, or using slang words. Though speaking should be conversational, it should not be as casual as you might be with friends. Consider who is in your audience and what language is appropriate for them. This also means that it may be appropriate to use more technical language before an expert audience. Never use complicated or technical language just to sound clever though. Only use it if it is necessary.

Avoid Filler Words

Filler words are words (or noises) that speakers make that are unnecessary and usually are just filling the space while the speaker tries to think of what to say next.

Example: "You know" is infectious

Once, I remember chatting with a friend and afterward, I noticed I was saying "you know" in almost every sentence! Then I realized that my friend was saying it in every sentence which was unlike her. We discovered that she had talked that afternoon with her sister who had been saying it constantly. That is when I realized that filler words are like contagious diseases that spread from person to person. This is because a natural part of speaking a language is to copy others and how they use it. I believe this makes us fit in and seem like part of the group but this is not helpful when speaking on the stage.

Filler words come in three strains of disease (which sometimes overlap and mix together):

- **Unnecessary noises**. "Er, um, ah, erm." These are just noises that add nothing to your speech. They are commonplace in normal conversation with another person because they act as a placeholder that informs them that we have not yet finished our thought and it is not their turn to jump in just yet. On stage, however, no one should be interrupting you so there is no need for such noise. This is important because these unnecessary noises can make a speaker seem unconfident. They can also be very annoying to the audience, especially if uttered every third word!

- **Misused words**. "... like ... you know ..." These words usually have no place in a sentence and are just adding noise in word form. Obviously, you can still use these words correctly but if you listen carefully to people speaking, you will realize that most of the time they use these, they are not describing something they like or know! Two more examples here would be "Sooooo ..." (to start a sentence) and "... aaaaaaannd ..." to join two sentences. These words might be technically correct but they are being used to give thinking time here when a pause would be better.

- **Overused words**. "So, basically, the thing is …" Anything that you overuse or rely on too much can become a filler word. I love starting sentences with "so" but if I do it all the time then it is a filler word. At college, I noticed a lot of people started sentences with "basically" because I think they thought it made them sound like they knew what they were talking about! A few years ago, I was infected by "the thing is …" though, in my defense, I noticed journalists on TV and online were also overusing it at the same time.

One tip to avoid using filler words is to slow down when speaking so that you have a more reasonable pace to think about what you are saying. A brief pause instead of a filler word will be all you need.

Another tip is to be aware of what filler words you are using in your daily life and try to eliminate them. Though you are unlikely to completely eliminate them, be aware that the more you use them generally, the harder it will be to control them when speaking in public. Overall, I have built up a good immunity to most filler words, especially when speaking in public. One reason is that as soon as my wife or I become aware of a new filler word infection, I start fighting it. Currently, I'm fighting a battle against the word "whatever" and trying to stop myself from using it in everyday speech!

Toastmasters meetings have a dedicated "ah-counter" whose job it is to count all these filler words and report back how many times different people used them. The idea is not to humiliate the speakers but rather to provide them with a useful diagnosis of what filler word diseases they have. This is always useful information.

Body Language

Aside from using your voice, your body language is the other way that you are communicating with your audience. Body language is undoubtedly important though it is NOT responsible for 93% of all communication.* Here are the main aspects of body language, listed in what I believe is their order of importance:

Eye Contact

You were probably taught at a young age how important it is to look at people when you are speaking to them or they are speaking to you. It should come as no surprise that the same is true in public speaking. The two big benefits of looking at members of your audience in the eye are that it builds trust and credibility in you and it allows you to monitor your audience to see if they are following you. If they are not following you, it is an opportunity to adjust your delivery, engage their attention, or explain something in a different way. Eye contact also personalizes your talk. Though you may have a big audience, you usually want each person to feel

---

* This is the often-quoted but wrong "Mehrabian Myth" which misinterprets Albert Mehrabian's 1967 psychology study about inconsistent communications. That study found that where words, speaker tone, and speaker expressions were inconsistent, audiences relied on them in the following amounts to understand the speaker's true meaning: words 7%, tone 38%, and expression 55%. A classic example of this would be asking your partner if they are still angry at you and they reply, "NO!" while scowling with crossed arms! You will believe their tone and expression instead of their word. The study is important however for showing that your body language should be consistent with what you are saying.

that you are speaking to them individually. (This is part of the audience connection discussed in Chapter 5.)

- **Where do you look?** It may seem obvious, but you actually have to look into a person's eyes! I remember an early speech I gave at Toastmasters where my evaluator noticed that I was looking just above the audience's eyes. Looking in the general direction was not good enough. I needed to make actual eye contact.

- **How long do you look?** Eye contact is not a staring contest, so don't look at someone too long or you will make them uncomfortable. Look at someone for a few sentences or while making a point and then move on to another person.

- **What if I'm scared?** Looking at people directly can be nerve-wracking, especially if you are shy or introverted. It is nevertheless essential and you may have to treat it as part of your "fake it till you make it" aspect of confidence. The problem, if you do not look at people, is that you may look nervous, untrustworthy (e.g., if you look to the ceiling), or bored, (e.g., if you look at the floor).

- **Find the friendly faces (and ignore the scary ones)!** As you look around your audience and make eye contact, some faces will be smiling and will seem friendlier than others. Use these as your anchor points that you can keep coming back to as they will give you confidence. Conversely, you may find people whose expressions seem unfriendly. For the most part, you want to ignore these. You do not know what might be happening in their lives that may be affecting them at the moment. Often, you will be surprised afterward to find that these people were enjoying your speech.

- **What if there are too many people?** In a big audience, you cannot look at every individual so try to spread around where you look. Don't focus on just one side or section of the audience. You may be able to look into the eyes of individuals in the front but may have to look more generally toward the people in the back. Remember the goal is to make sure that no one feels left out.

Facial Expression

Facial expression plays a big part in how your audience will react to you. For the most part, you will want to be smiling and friendly. If you do this naturally, you are very lucky and audiences will easily warm to you. Try to be aware of your facial expressions. For example, I have a tendency not to smile when I'm concentrating. This means if I'm giving a new speech, I may not be smiling if I'm trying too hard. Therefore, I remind myself to smile and sometimes even write it on my notes!

We mentioned the importance of varying your emotions as you speak (see Vocal Variety above). The important thing to remember is that your expression should (roughly) match what you are talking about. It sounds obvious, but this is a skill that many new speakers struggle with initially because of all the skills they are trying to master at the same time. If you were talking about the death of someone, it would be inappropriate to have a beaming smile on your face. Now, this does not mean you need to give an Oscar-winning performance breaking down in tears either, but you should be appropriately somber. Another classic mismatch is when someone talks about something new and exciting and they sound and look bored. Their expression needs to convey some of their excitement.

Hands

A lot of new speakers find knowing what to do with their hands the hardest. To start with, just putting your hands by your side is probably the most natural thing to do. Gradually as you become more experienced you may notice ways you use them, such as when you are more animated. Try to observe how you use your hands when speaking casually. The main goal is simply to remain natural and not distracting with your hands.

There are a few things you should not do with your hands. Don't put them in your pockets because it is distracting or looks like you don't care. Don't fold your arms because that is a barrier between you and your audience. Don't cover your groin area with your hands because it looks like you are a defender protecting yourself from a soccer kick! If possible, don't hold notes. First, notes risk blocking the audience's view of you. Secondly, the paper will amplify any nervous shaking you may be experiencing and this could also be distracting if it makes a noise.

Feet

What you do with your feet will depend on whether you have a stage to move around or if you are standing behind a lectern. If you have a choice, I'd recommend coming out from behind a lectern because it can act as a barrier between you and your audience. In case you're thinking, "a shield to protect me from the audience sounds great!" remember that you want to be as open as you can to your audience so that they trust and like you and your message.

In the past, a lot has been made of so-called "power poses" (such as standing facing the audience with your legs in a wide stance). It is certainly good to face your audience and not turn from them but otherwise, I think the most important factor is that you look natural. Any unnatural pose risks looking ridiculous.

If you are moving around the stage, try to do it with purpose. This means don't just pace backward and forward (like some college professors do) as this is distracting. Move to an area of the stage and make a point. Then move a little to another area and make another point. One of the golden rules of speaking is not to distract the audience, so another thing to avoid is any bouncing motion up and down or awkward foot movement that may take away from your speech.

Clothing

Similarly, with clothing, make sure that what you are wearing does not distract the audience either by its look or because it is hindering your ability to speak comfortably, or because it interferes with a microphone. Obviously, if your clothing (such as a particular costume) is part of your speech then that is a different situation.

4.3 Delivery

The delivery of your speech is the main event (and maybe the reason you got this book). However, most of what you need to do has already been covered in the practice section above. This section just considers how the aspects of speaking in public during your actual event may be different from practice.

How is Delivery Different From Practice?

You Only Get One Chance

This is it. No matter how perfect you'd like your speech to be, it probably won't be. Don't worry. But whatever you do now, the show must go on. That means that if something doesn't happen as you wish, you cannot stop and start again. You must carry on as any professional performer would do.

> **Example: The time the show stopped**
>
> One of the most excruciating experiences of my life was watching my sister's violin teacher stop elementary school students in the middle of a solo concert performance to draw attention to every mistake they made. The poor students were alone on stage as the teacher asked them in front of everyone, "Now, what did you do wrong?" Worse still, she then made them start from the beginning again! It was agony for everyone and it felt like it went on forever.

If you make a mistake and it's noticed then own it. It will make you more human and sympathetic to your audience. Often it may not even be noticed. I've had speeches where I've forgotten things I wished to say but no one ever knew. Sometimes I've done something accidentally but the audience thought it was deliberate. As long as you're in control (or look like you're in control), it doesn't matter.

Energy

You sometimes hear speakers talk about being present or in the moment on stage. Your energy levels are likely to be significantly higher than for a mere practice. Think about where you are on the Speaker Nerves Spectrum (see Chapter 2) and adjust accordingly. This is also why you hear some people say (misguidedly) that there is no point in practicing because you cannot replicate the real thing. While it is true that the real event is different, the point is that the more you have practiced, the better able you will be to deal with the real moment on stage.

Breathing

Remember to keep breathing properly and use breathing to calm you down, before and during your speech. Before going on stage, a simple method to calm yourself is to breathe in through your nose for three seconds and out through your mouth for three seconds and repeat this. On stage, before starting your speech, as you take a moment to look around you can also take some good breaths. Smile as you do this so you look relaxed and confident.

Adjust in Real-Time

As you speak before your real audience, you will be getting feedback in real-time according to how they respond and react to your speech. The best thing you can do is adjust to this. You might change your energy levels or give the audience more or less of something they want.

Personalize

You may be giving a speech that you have given to many audiences but you do not want it to seem impersonal. You can personalize a speech by interacting with your audience. You can look at them and seek validation for your points or ask for their thoughts. You might have spoken to some of them before and be able to bring them or their ideas into your speech. You might be able to refer to something that has happened at the venue or their organization or something in the news currently that they are all aware of. Anything you can do to personalize it will make you connect better with them.

Example: Be real, not a video

I once spent a morning watching a professional speaker who is recognized as being at the top of the speaking profession. While his speech was excellent, I was surprised and disappointed that at no point did he personalize any of it to the audience in the room. We might as well have been watching a video.

Improvise

This is not for everyone but it is one of my favorite aspects of speaking. When I am in the moment on stage, I find that my brain is very active. I often get ideas that I've never had before. It might be an example or analogy I can use to illustrate a point I'm making. I like doing this because it is usually obvious that I'm personalizing my speech. Though an improvised idea will not be well practiced, it will appear fresher (and perhaps more exciting) to your audience. If the audience likes it, you should consider incorporating it into your talk in the future. Improvisation often works well with humor too. If something funny happens (or occurs to you), a simple improvised comment in the moment can be highly effective.

Example: A bird breaks the tension

When I was a teacher, I remember our new principal addressing all the staff one week after he took over. Tension was high among the teachers as many changes were being introduced at the school. As the principal spoke, a bird somehow got into the hall and was distracting everyone as it flew around. I called out, "This never happened with the last principal!" and everyone (including the new principal) burst out laughing. An improvised thought in the moment shattered the tension and everyone appreciated it.

Just because you are good at improvising though should not be an excuse to avoid practice. If you make everything up (or "just wing it") your speech will not be as well structured or clear. In Speech Map terms, you risk not getting to your destination or not getting there efficiently. When your speech is well structured (namely, you know where you are going and how to get there), an improvised moment is like spotting a scenic view en route. You can spend a few moments there before carrying on to your destination.

Time

Time is more important when you deliver your speech than when you practice because you only get one chance to get it right. This means you must manage your time. No matter how much you have practiced, there is always a chance that your speech is faster or slower than in practice. This might be because of how quickly (or slowly) you are speaking or because of the audience's reaction (such as laughing or applauding). There are two main ways you can control the timing of your speech:

- **Monitor the time.** You want to be aware of the time throughout your speech. You should have a clear sense of what time you should be arriving at different sections. You may want to write these times next to any notes you have so you can quickly assess if you are ahead or behind. If you are slightly ahead or behind, you can then make small adjustments to your speech to get back on track.
- **Keep your speech flexible.** Your speech should be well structured and practiced enough that there are no big timing surprises when you deliver it. However, there may be times when you find that the timing of your speech needs a bigger adjustment. Examples might be:
    - You start late (through no fault of your own) but are expected to finish on time.
    - The organizer asks you to speak for longer or shorter than planned.

- The audience is particularly engaged in part of your speech (asking questions) and you spend more time on something than you intended to.
- The audience quickly understands your points and you find yourself moving through your material faster than expected.

If you need to shorten your speech, you may need to cut out a section or part of a section. To do this, you should be aware of how important each part of your speech is and how much time will be saved. The solution will require that you still make it to your speech destination. Note that it is never a good idea to finish a speech overtime. The audience is likely to lose interest as their minds start to focus on whatever they had planned next. By contrast, audiences are usually appreciative if you finish slightly early as you are giving them back some of their time.

If you find yourself needing to fill a more significant amount of time, you can use additional stories or examples. You can also allow the audience to ask questions or you can plan an activity for them to complete. Ideally, you should have these prepared beforehand so that you are ready to use them if needed rather than trying to create them in the moment.

Space

Usually, the space in which you are speaking will be bigger than where you practice (unless you have had the advantage of practicing in the same place where you will be delivering your speech). This means you should think about how you will use your speaking area. If the stage is big, will you move around so that you do not look like you are stuck in one place? Have you checked out different corners of the room where the audience will be sitting so that you can appreciate their view of you on stage? The more that you can use the stage, the more you will appear to be in control.

Questions and Answers (Q&A)

Many speaking events will feature Q&A. Here are some important considerations:

- **When to allow them?** Many top speaker coaches recommend incorporating Q&A into the middle of your speech so that it is not left until the end. The reason for this is that it allows you to have complete control over the end of your speech and finish with a strong, impactful close. If you have this choice, then by all means take it. You may find however that the expectation is that you allow questions at the end. The advantage of this is that the audience will have heard the whole of your presentation so you may have answered some questions they previously had. As a question period is more flexible, you can also use this as a buffer should you experience any of the timing issues mentioned above.

- **Repeat the question.** This is particularly important if a questioner is not using a microphone. Just as it is crucial that an audience can hear you speak, it is equally important that they can hear any questions you are answering. Repeating the question allows the audience to hear what was asked. It also gives you some time to start thinking about your answer and is a chance to confirm to the questioner that you have understood the question.

- **Answer the question!** There is nothing more annoying than a person who avoids answering a question (which is why watching politicians can be very frustrating). Unless there is an issue of confidentiality, don't avoid answering a question you have been asked. Even if the answer is a difficult or unpopular one, the audience will appreciate your honesty which in turn will go toward your credibility as a trustworthy expert. If you divert away from the question to answer something else then you either appear untrustworthy or less of an expert for not understanding the question.

- **What if I don't know the answer?** The one time it is acceptable not to answer the question is if you do not know the answer. In this case, give the best answer you can and explain what you don't know (and if appropriate, why you don't know it). Honesty will boost your credibility with the audience. If possible, you should look to follow up with an answer after the event is over.

- **What if I don't get any questions?** Audiences can sometimes need a little warming up to think of questions during a Q&A period. If you face silence after asking if there are any questions, you can start by answering a question you often receive: "One of the most common questions I get asked is …" This helps the audience with useful information and gives them time to start thinking of their own questions.

What if Something Goes Wrong?

The worry of something going wrong is likely to arise long before you speak and as a result, we looked at this in Chapter 2 (Confidence).

Final Thoughts – Two Checklists

By now you will realize that speaking successfully involves lots of moving parts and things to consider. You may find it helpful to have checklists to help you remember everything you need to do. Below are two checklists you can adapt as necessary.

CHECKLIST FOR BEFORE SPEAKING	Done?
Logistics • Make travel arrangements, get tickets, etc. • Do you know where you're going? • Do you know when you need to be there? • Do you need to bring materials, equipment, with you? • Have you checked your stage/speaking area?	
Organizer • Have you met the organizer and checked anything you or they need to know before speaking? • Have you given them your speaker introduction? • Have you given them a copy of any slides or handouts to distribute?	
Audiovisual • Have you checked your slides work? • Have you checked the microphone? • Do you have a way to check the time while you are speaking?	
You (the speaker) • Have you warmed up your voice? • Do you have water available? • Do you have your Speech Map/notes? • Are you dressed comfortably and appropriately?	
Audience • Do you know who will be in the audience? • Have you met or spoken to any of them? • Can you refer to them in your speech?	

CHECKLIST FOR AFTER SPEAKING	Done?
• Have you thanked the organizer? • Have you provided any information (or answers to questions) you agreed to give after the event? • Have you received feedback from the organizer/participants? • Will there be future opportunities for speaking? • Have you connected with people you met at the event?	

CHAPTER 5
CONNECTION

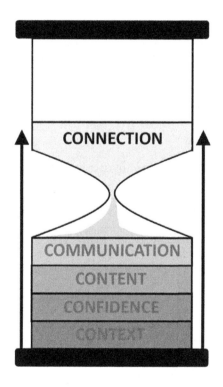

In this chapter...

If you have followed this book up to this point, you should have everything you need to give a good speech. The advice in this chapter is about standing out and taking it to the next level. Obviously, this is not necessary if you are just trying to survive a presentation! However, if you want to give the very best speech you can, this chapter will give you some useful tools. If Chapter 3 showed you how to take your audience to your speech destination, this chapter will show you how to take them there in style.

The secret to a great speech is to have a great connection with your audience. From their perspective, a speech should not be a passive experience with words that are just read out to them. They should be fully engaged on the journey you are taking them on. While you will always be able to make a speech better, I've set out below what I think are the eight biggest game changers.

Speech Return on Investment (Speech ROI)

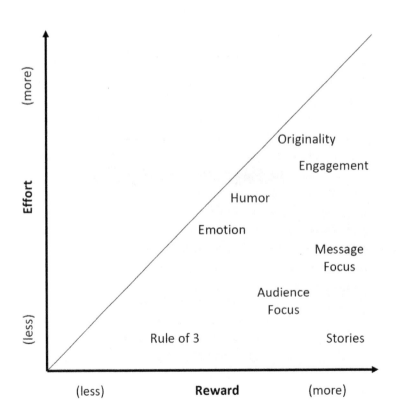

All of these game changers can have a big impact on connecting with your audience. The Speech Return on Investment chart shows my (rough) view of how much effort they require and how much reward you can get from each of these. They are all game changers because the rewards to your speech outweigh the effort they require. You will realize that there is also some overlap between some of these. An original, funny, emotional story that emphasizes your message for the audience's benefit covers six of these! Nevertheless, we'll consider each separately.

5.1 Stories

If you want the maximum reward for the minimum effort, the first element to work on in speaking is your stories. By stories, I don't mean, "Once upon a time …" but rather the stories and experiences of your life. These involve less effort because you have all the material already. You have already lived through these experiences (and probably already told people about them).

Why Stories?

There are two main reasons why storytelling is the perfect way to connect with audiences. First, we have spent our whole lives listening to stories. They are ever-present in our lives, whether they are entertainment (films, tv, books) or social (news, gossip, social media). Even before humans had ways of recording stories, they passed them on through storytelling. Listening to and telling stories is simply part of the human condition. That means that one of the best things to do to get an audience interested in your speech is to tell stories because everyone loves a good story.

The second reason stories are great in speeches is an advantage for you, the speaker. If you are telling something that has happened to you, you already know it. You don't need to try to remember it from notes. You can simply relive the experience which is what we all do every day when we tell friends and family about things that have happened to us. Assuming the story is your own, you are also the expert on it, increasing your credibility with the audience.

Guide to Storytelling

We are all naturally better storytellers than we might realize. Whenever you tell friends, family, and colleagues a story about something that happened to you, you are probably used to making it interesting. If it's boring, they won't want to listen! Often you might be competing for attention with other people so you have to catch their attention quickly and hold it. You might be used to exaggerating aspects of the story or dramatizing aspects of it to get a reaction from people. All of these skills are useful when you are telling a story in your speech. You can use everyday storytelling both to practice stories and see which stories get the best reaction from the people you tell. Below are some top tips for telling gripping stories.

Tell a Personal Story

Preferably, you should tell your own stories because you are the expert on them and this will also minimize the chances of the audience having heard them before. When audiences hear famous stories repeated, they are more likely to lose interest and question the credibility of the speaker. If you cannot find a personal story to illustrate a point but you have an example of a perfect story that happened to someone else, at least see if you can add a personal analysis to it to make it unique. What did you do or how did your life change after you heard that story?

The Basics

Just as we learn to write stories with plot, characters, and setting, so your story should usually answer the following questions:

- Who is in it? (Characters)
- Where and when does it take place? (Setting)
- What happens? (Plot)

Structure

The stories in your speech are not trying to become a prize-winning novel but there should be a structure to them that makes sense to the audience. It rarely makes sense to confuse the audience, and if you do (deliberately), you usually want to clear it up very quickly. Your story should have a beginning, middle, and end and these should be clear. You do not necessarily have to present the story in this order but it should be clear to the audience what is happening.

Some speakers choose to start a story halfway through at a moment of drama (much like a TV show). This is good for grabbing the audience's attention, but make sure you don't leave them confused. You may subsequently need to go back to the beginning to explain how you got to that point. Use your structure to present all the information that the audience needs.

Sometimes speakers might split a story up. After reaching a point of climax, they delay the ending to continue with their speech. This can work well to hold the audience's curiosity and attention. It is also effective with powerful stories that you want to end your speech with.

A similar structural technique that is very powerful is the callback. A callback is where you refer back to something that happened or was said earlier. There is something very satisfying to a listener about remembering where you started as you arrive at the end of a story. An example of this might be a story that begins and ends in the same place or with the same characters doing the same thing. The callback should be both a memory of what came before and also have moved the audience on with new knowledge that they didn't possess at the beginning of the story. Incidentally, callbacks work very well within the structure of a speech too.

Dialogue

Dialogue can have a magical effect on stories by bringing them to life. When asked to tell a story, the vast majority of people narrate it in the past tense. Creating dialogue between characters allows you to transport the audience to the actual event in real-time.

Example: Narration vs. dialogue

Past tense narration:

"I went nervously into my boss's office and asked for a pay rise. He stared at me for what seemed like an age and then fired me on the spot."

Present tense dialogue:

[*Walk into boss's office nervously.*]

"Sir?"

"Yes, what is it?"

"Well ..."

"Hurry up!"

"Well as you know, I'm on the same salary as when I joined ten years ago. My wife's just had a baby and I was wondering if I could have a pay rise?"

... [*Boss glares*]

"NO! You're fired! Get out!"

The dialogue conveys so much more information than the narrative. It also greatly increases the tension in the scene. The problem with narrating stories can be that even big moments are glossed over with minimal emotion.

You may be wondering how you can do dialogue if you are only one speaker. The answer is that you can become both characters. The simplest way to do this is to be one character in a space on the stage and then be the other character a step away from them. That way you are performing the characters in different places and the audience will recognize them. You are not trying to be an Oscar-winning actor but you can also have fun distinguishing between the characters if they have different voices, mannerisms, or physical characteristics. For example, in a dialogue between a child and an adult (both played by you), as the child, you would look up at the adult and as the adult, you would look down at the child.

Characters

Your story will usually have characters other than you. Try to help the audience understand who they are whether by describing them and their motivations or portraying them in dialogue (see above). It helps if the audience can identify with them and in particular you want the audience to root for the hero of the story.

Don't be the Hero of Your Own Story

Speaking of heroes, it is best if you are not the hero of your own story. This avoids the audience thinking that you are arrogant or boastful and makes it easier for them to root for the hero. If your story is about something you achieved, perhaps the hero is the person that helped you achieve it. Kids make wonderful heroes because (almost!) everyone is sympathetic to kids.

Present Tense

Because your stories necessarily occurred in the past, it is natural to describe them in the past tense. However, it will be more exciting for your audience if you can relive the stories in the present. Using dialogue (see above) makes this easy. You can also describe a scene in the present tense.

Example: The employee again

Here is the employee from the story above narrating in the present tense:

"Imagine you're there with me, standing outside my boss's office. His assistant is nowhere to be seen. Through the door, I hear him shouting down the phone at some poor soul. Should I knock?"

Tension

A story without tension or conflict is a boring story. A lot of stories naturally have tension in them but speakers breeze over the moment toward an easy resolution. The problem with this is that the struggle does not seem like a big one and the solution or lesson learned does not seem profound. At the same time, you risk your audience's minds relaxing too soon and beginning to wander. When you have a moment of genuine tension, make sure that you extract the most from it. Can you heighten it or extend it? The use of pauses can dramatically increase tension and suspense.

Make sure your expressions and emotions when telling this part of a story are consistent with what is happening. You do not want to be smiling when describing a terrifying moment because it will not seem terrifying.

Resolve Questions

This advice is generally true of your speech, but especially so within stories. Do not leave the audience with unresolved questions in their head because this will distract and frustrate them. Who is that character? Why are they doing that? What is it? Where are they going? The worst mistake is not finishing the story. Even if the ending isn't the point you want to make, you still need to finish it off.

Example: What happened to the employee?

Remember our poor employee from the story above? Imagine a speaker used the story from this section about entering the boss's office to show how to overcome anxiety. By using the techniques the speaker listed, he built up the courage to knock on the door and ask his boss for a pay rise. Regardless of how that conversation subsequently went and how relevant it is to your point, you have to tell the audience about it because every single one of them will be thinking, "What happened next? How did it go?"

5.2 Audience Focus

Focusing on your audience seems obvious and indeed it has featured throughout the stages of this book that have led us to this point. To start with, the context stage required identifying what you needed to do to make sure your speech met your audience's needs. In the confidence stage, we saw that focusing on the audience rather than yourself was the biggest way to gain confidence. In the content stage, we used the Value Filter and Interest Filter which were designed to identify messages that would benefit your audience. The Speech Map process is designed to create the clearest possible outline of your speech that will make it easier for audiences to understand. In the delivery stage, we discussed the importance of personalizing your speech for your audience. Here are further general tips to help focus on the audience:

I vs. You

A very simple way to determine how focused you are on your audience is to look at the ratio between the times you say "I" and "you" in your speech. Naturally, you will need to use "I" to introduce yourself and describe things you have done, but if the whole speech overuses it then it is likely a speech more about you than one of benefit to your audience. Try to limit your use of "I" and focus on your audience by asking them questions or putting them in the position of implementing your message. When you use "you" or "your" it will be more engaging for the audience. Throughout this book, though I have referred to my stories and experiences ("I"), I have used "you" and "your" a lot because you are the one who will be speaking and this book is to help you.

Speak to One and Look to All

This is a very clever piece of advice I first heard from Toastmasters World Champions of Public Speaking Craig Valentine and Darren LaCroix. The idea is that though you are speaking to an audience as a whole, you should be addressing each person as an individual in that audience as if you were talking to them alone. Typically, this is done by using "you" instead of "all of you." Another example is to ask a question to an individual rather than to a group. For example, say, "Have you ever done something amazing?" not, "How many of you have ever done something amazing?" The former question is personalized to the listener whereas the latter question draws attention to the fact that the listener is in a big audience.

Occasionally you may want to draw attention to everyone in the audience if your point is to highlight a fact or statistic about them or if you wish to avoid offending or embarrassing audience members. For example, "We all spend too much time watching TV, don't we?"

Know Your Audience

There are two ways to know your audience. You can know specific people in the audience or you can know the general type of audience you have in front of you. You may know people specifically because they are your friends and colleagues but if not, you can get to know them either by meeting them at the event before you speak or even conducting interviews with some of them in the weeks before you speak. (You can ask the event organizer for names of people you can interview to find out more about their issues that you are addressing in your speech.) Once you know people, you can refer to them by name in your speech to highlight their concerns or experiences.

It is useful to know your general type of audience so you can adjust your message and delivery accordingly. A friendly audience will require less convincing than a hostile audience which may need to be treated more cautiously. A tired audience may need more energy from you to wake them up and engage them.

Tell the Audience How They Benefit

In the first few minutes of a speech, one way to convince audience members that they made a good decision coming to hear you speak is to let them know how they will benefit by listening to you. This is often called "WIIFM" ("What's In It For Me?") and is a key strategy that marketers everywhere use. Not only does this make the people in the audience feel good about being there, but it also arouses their curiosity and keeps them interested. Focus on the benefits they will get rather than just describing the features of what you are talking about. If you feel that listing all the benefits upfront gets in the way of how you like to start your speech, then you could either have them listed by the person who introduces you, or else you should make sure you mention them early on in your speech.

Don't Alienate Your Audience

There are two main ways to alienate your audience. The first is to talk about something in which they have no interest. An example would be having an audience that is split roughly 50-50 between men and women but talking about something which overwhelmingly interests or affects only one gender. The solution in this case is either to pick a better topic or to come at the topic from both a male and female perspective.*

The second way to alienate your audience is to offend them.

Example: The danger of politics

In a speech in America, I once told a childhood story and made a joke about Margaret Thatcher, the former Conservative British Prime Minister. Even though this was a single comment about an event from another country 25 years previously, I received feedback that my speech was way too liberal! Clearly, some subjects, such as politics, are always going to entail a degree of risk. Of course, if politics is your job you may be unable to avoid speaking about it but you can still assess your audience and control the risk of offending them.

You may also have difficult news to share with your audience that may be unpopular. The best advice in these situations is to be upfront about bad news and as honest and sympathetic as possible. The more you model this, the greater your credibility will be.

---

* A wonderful example of this is speaker Mark Gungor (markgungor.com) who speaks hilariously about marital relationships from both the male and female perspectives.

Give the Audience What They Want

This is particularly important where the audience may have certain expectations of you. If you are known for something or have a certain classic story, the audience may want you to do it and may be disappointed if you don't.

Example: Queen at Live Aid

Though not a speech, there are some useful lessons from studying a performance of the rock band Queen. Over the course of 20 minutes on a July night in 1985, Queen gave what is widely considered the greatest rock performance of all time. On the day itself, 75 of the world's most famous singers and groups were performing in London and Philadelphia. How did Queen manage to outshine all of them?

Content

The key factor that made Queen stand out was that they thought about their audience and put them first. Specifically, they considered what would give their audience the best possible time that they could have in 20 minutes. Queen's answer was to play songs that the audience would want to hear (greatest hits) and which would involve them the most (engagement). Instead of playing three or four songs in 20 minutes like other groups, they cut their songs to fit six in as well as Freddie Mercury's trademark a cappella call-and-response with the crowd section. Here is their set list:

- **"Bohemian Rhapsody"** - first part only; their greatest hit gets the crowd instantly on their side.
- **"Radio Gaga"** - a newer song, but an anthem made for large crowds to clap their hands together.
- **"Ay-Oh"** - Freddie addresses the crowd and involves them singing along with him.
- **"Hammer to Fall"** - another newer song.

- **"Crazy Little Thing Called Love"** - Freddie dedicates the song to the crowd and compliments them. At one point in the song, Freddie falls silent and conducts the audience through singing the chorus.
- **"We Will Rock You"** - shortened; the ultimate stadium anthem for the crowd to join in.
- **"We Are The Champions"** - another stadium anthem leaving the crowd feeling uplifted.

Delivery

Queen and Freddie Mercury were always great performers. Here are some techniques they used to make the performance so memorable:

- **High Energy** – Freddie brought high energy to the stage and played to the crowd. There was no time (or need) in the 20-minute set for slowing down. In their longer concerts, they naturally had slower, quieter moments. Queen actually returned to the stage later that night to play a more poignant, slower song ("Is This The World We Created ...?").
- **Engagement and interactivity** – As shown above, the crowd were involved in most of the songs and actively encouraged by Freddie throughout.
- **Personalization** – In "We Are The Champions," there is a line, "You brought me fame and fortune and everything that goes with it. *I thank you all.*" Freddie didn't sing that last sentence but spoke it as if he was saying it personally to the audience. The audience understood this nuance and screamed and applauded as he said it.
- **Adapting** – The Queen band members were in the audience as some of the earlier acts played and noticed that the music was not very loud. Queen's sound engineer turned up the sound levels when they played so that they were louder than anyone else and dominated the stadium.

How could you use these techniques to rock your next speech?!

5.3 Message Focus

Your message clarity and focus should be a top priority for your speech. If you followed the Speech Map process in Chapter 3 then you should already have a very focused message. Message Focus still appears here as an advanced skill because every decision you make about what to do or not to do in your speech should be run through a filter of whether or not it makes your message clearer.

What do You Want the Audience to Remember?

You will know from your own experience that it is hard to remember information. It is well known that after hearing new information, we forget a lot of it very quickly. The amount we forget also increases with time unless we do something to help our memory such as refresh it or write down what is important. This presents speakers with a paradox. The more information you present, the more your audience will forget![*]

It is therefore very important not to give too much information in your presentation. Some inexperienced speakers try to overcome their fear of having nothing to say by saying everything they know about a subject. This is not helpful. As we saw in the content chapter, you want to have an overall message and some key points that lead you there. These should be what you want the audience to remember.

How Can You Get the Audience to Remember?

- **Limit the points that you make.** A good rule of thumb in a longer speech is to make about one point every ten minutes. Therefore, if you are speaking for 30 minutes, you should aim to make about three main points.

---

[*] This is the key point I want you to remember. For that reason, I haven't included research about the Forgetting Curve. I'm certainly not going to mention that Hermann Ebbinghaus invented it in 1885. Oops, too late! Please forget this unimportant information and go back and read my main point!

- **Limit your facts and statistics.** Many presenters love facts and statistics. Many audiences hate them! In my experience, it is exceedingly rare for an audience to love a fact or statistic as much as the presenter does. For that reason, it is essential for a presenter to focus on only the most important statistics and facts.
- **Emphasize the key points.** Don't mumble through the most important part of your speech. Create a fanfare! Sound the sirens! Make sure the audience knows how important your point is.
- **Repeat your key points**. You're not testing and grading your audience and it's not a competition! Make it easy for them and repeat the key information.
- **Display the key points.** Write them down on a slide (one per slide) or handout.
- **Make the key points memorable**. Connect them to a story or picture or feeling the audience has. If the audience remembers that, it will help them remember the key point.

What do You Want the Audience to do?

Not every speech has to have a call to action, but a lot of the time there will be something that the audience can do next. Make it easy for the audience by telling them what they can do next and make it as easy as possible for them to do. That motivation to act that an audience member has at the end of your presentation can quickly be lost as they return to their normal lives and all the distractions and demands on them. Can they do something while they are still in the room with you (such as signing up to connect with you or scanning a QR code for more information)? Will you (or an organizer) be able to follow up with them soon to help them achieve their next step? Never leave the audience guessing what they are supposed to do next.

Translate Facts and Statistics

Facts and statistics are much better understood by audiences when they are translated by a presenter in such a way that gives them context.

Example: Find a number the audience can relate to

Instead of saying, "609,360 deaths from cancer are expected to occur in the US this year," you could translate it to:

- "Imagine losing the whole population of Vermont this year to cancer."
- "Imagine losing the whole population of [Louisville, Kentucky] [Pittsburg, twice over] this year to cancer."
- "In the next hour, while I'm speaking, 70 Americans will die from cancer."
- "Every minute I'm on this stage, another American has died from cancer."

Obviously, this is a grim example. But the danger with the original statistic is that it is boring and unrelatable.

If you want to motivate your audience to take action, you have to find a way to present the statistic so it means something to them.

5.4 Engagement

If you have followed everything up to this point in the book, your speech content should be engaging. Nevertheless, it is always worth considering how you can make your speech more engaging and interesting to the audience. The essence of engagement in this section is to take the audience from a passive experience to an active, memorable one. This requires a bit more effort on your part but it will greatly reward your speech.

Curiosity

Curiosity is the key to engagement. If you make an audience curious you engage their brain and they want to learn more. Curiosity can even start before your speech by advertising your speech or with a speech title. "The one secret to becoming rich," is a much more curiosity-provoking speech title than "Sensible investment tips." It works because it promises something the audience wants (to get rich) and teases an answer to the question, "What's the secret?"

It makes sense to use curiosity as a hook early on (and throughout) your speech so that the audience knows they have to pay attention to get their reward. You can use curiosity by:

- Asking a question and teasing the answer.
- Starting a story, then waiting to reveal how it ends.
- Showing something new (for example, a product) and then creating anticipation about how it works or what it does. Steve Jobs was a master at this.
- Revealing how the audience will benefit from listening to you and getting them excited about the results before they know how.
- Revealing something surprising.

Curiosity is incredibly powerful. My children sometimes complain that their lessons at school are boring. It's not a feeling I particularly identify with because throughout my life, whenever I find myself in a boring lesson or presentation, I create my own curiosity to survive the experience! Typically, this means I start asking questions in my head about the subject matter and then wondering what the answers are. I then pay more attention to the speaker because I'm hoping they'll answer my questions. If they don't, I usually ask my questions. As a speaker, you don't want to rely on the audience having to create their own curiosity. Do it for them.

Demonstrations

Demonstrations can bring an idea or product to life, especially when they are relatively new or unusual. Pitches in TV shows such as *Shark Tank* or *Dragon's Den* often include demonstrations for this reason. A good demonstration taps into the curiosity (above) and different learning styles (below). If your demonstration can show the audience that something is easy (achievable) and can produce dramatic results then they will be hooked.

Visual, Auditory and Kinesthetic Learning

When teachers are training, they are taught that we all have different learning styles. Some people prefer:

- **Visual learning** – seeing and reading.
- **Auditory learning** – listening and speaking.
- **Kinesthetic learning** – touching and doing.

Teachers are therefore encouraged to deliver lessons that incorporate these different ways of learning. Speakers are in a similar position. If you just stand on stage talking to your audience, you may only be catering to the auditory learners. Here are some ways to enhance each learning type:

- **Visual learning**
    - Use slides and handouts.
    - Use videos and pictures.
    - Use props.
    - Act out scenes and dialogue on stage.
    - Use the stage purposefully (presenting different points in different places) and visually (e.g., a chronological speech could go from left to right for the audience like a timeline).
    - Paint a descriptive, visual picture in the minds of the audience.
- **Auditory learning**
    - Vary your voice (volume, tone, pace, emotion).
    - Play an audio track.
    - Play music or sing.
    - Get the audience to discuss something in pairs.
- **Kinesthetic learning**
    - Get the audience up and moving.
    - Get the audience to practice something.
    - Play games.
    - Work in groups on projects or challenges.

Ideas to enhance kinesthetic learning can be more challenging, especially with a large audience or where there is limited space to move. Nevertheless, they can provide tremendous energy to an audience and also work well as movement breaks to split up a presentation. Kinesthetic learning also works well in workshop situations.

Participation

The ultimate way to engage the audience is to have them participate in what you do. There are many ways to do this:

- **Questions** – Ask the whole audience a question and get them to answer together, or poll the audience ("by show of hands …").
- **Volunteers** – If you invite a volunteer on stage, the audience may feel that the volunteer represents them and gives them a stake in the activity, especially if the volunteer is well known to them.
- **Whole audience** – You can get a whole audience to do a movement or breathing exercise. One of my most memorable experiences was sitting in a lecture hall while a professor instructed different sections of the audience to make different noises (using items we had on us). He then conducted us in a piece of music, similar to the show *Stomp* which uses ordinary objects to make music.
- **Electronic participation** – Given that most people have smartphones now, you can interact with your audience in real-time electronically. They can tag your speech on social media. You can also use software programs to run quizzes that the audience can answer live on their phones.

5.5 Originality

Originality is another great way to connect with your audience. Being truly original requires hard work but it also promises great rewards and guarantees that your audience will remember you and your speech. This is particularly important at an event where you may be one of many speakers. How can you make sure that when the event is over, you are the one that the audience remembers?

We examined originality back with the Interest Filter in Chapter 3. It is harder to find original topics to speak about, but your stories, experiences, and delivery should be unique to you and are therefore the perfect opportunity to be original.

Message

Do you have an original message? It is unlikely that you have thought of something that no one else has before. However, perhaps you have a novel solution or approach to achieving the goal of your message. Perhaps your experience was unusual and makes you better qualified to deliver the message.

Stories

Even your personal stories can be familiar ones. I have heard many speeches from different people that told the same following story:

"My life was normal. I got cancer. I didn't think I could beat it. I beat it!"

If you are telling a familiar story you need to think about what details you can add to make it original, because otherwise, your audience will be ahead of you in knowing how the story ends. What made your situation unusual or funny or agony? Can you surprise the audience by making them think the story is going one way but then it goes another? Or can you take a familiar story and transplant it into a different setting? After all *West Side Story* is essentially *Romeo and Juliet,* but both are fantastic.

Personal Identity and Characteristics

Everyone is original. Perhaps you have a characteristic that makes you stand out from other speakers.

Example: Nick Vujicic

Australian speaker, Nick Vujicic, is a wonderful speaker but the most surprising thing to audiences who haven't seen him before is that he has no arms and legs! Early on in his speeches, he answers all the questions in the heads of audience members ("How did it happen? How do you move about?..."). That alone is not enough to make him a great speaker, but it does make him stand out. His content is amazing too.

You should think about how you stand out from your audience. As a white male, I am often in majority groups. However, as an elementary school teacher in America, when I spoke in front of the other teachers, I was in lots of minorities by being male, British, middle-aged, divorced, and a parent. Remember that while the point of being different is to stand out, to build a connection with your audiences you will want to show them how you are the same as them.

Presentation Style and Props

Do you present in a way that is unusual or do you have some props that are unique to you? In the same way that a new product should ideally have a unique selling point, what is your USP? Remember to avoid gimmicks. The objective is to help the audience remember you and your message.

5.6 Humor

Just about any speech can be made better with humor. Even the darkest moments in our lives can be filled with black humor and the saying, "I didn't know whether to laugh or cry" shows just how close the two emotions can be. Humor is great because it entertains the audience and wakes them up. The act of laughing is infectious. An audience that is laughing and enjoying your speech will be connecting with you and your message.

Speakers also have a big advantage over comedians. Usually, the audience has not paid money to come and see you make them laugh. Any laughter should therefore be an unexpected bonus from their perspective.

Humor is not the same as telling jokes. Unless you are masterful at telling jokes, I strongly advise against it. The problem with jokes is that they risk being unfunny, corny, offensive, unoriginal, and irrelevant to your speech. You also have to remember them and deliver them well.

On the other hand, humor mostly consists of seeing the funny side of things. As a result, you can be humorous throughout your speech in ways that seem natural, spontaneous, relevant, and without high stakes. A joke has high stakes in the sense that you are thinking, "Here comes the punchline. I hope the audience laughs." With humor, you can say something funny and it doesn't matter if only a few people find it funny. You will notice many comedians use this approach (and the ideas below) rather than simply telling jokes.

Here are some ways to uncover humor in situations and see the funny side of things:

Be Self-Deprecating

This is a great place to start. You want to make your audience laugh but you don't want to risk offending them. How do you know what will offend them if you don't know them? Make fun of yourself! This works well if you have a particular trait or characteristic that the audience may be wondering about. You can use it as an icebreaker at the beginning of your speech to tell the audience a bit more about you while also making them laugh.

Example: The way I speak

Near the beginning of speeches to new audiences, I often say, "You can tell from my accent that I was born here in [Boston]!" because this acknowledges the question in the heads of the audience members about where I'm from while giving the audience a chance to laugh at my funny British accent.

Common Experience

The ultimate way to connect with an audience is through the humor of a shared experience. If something funny happened at an event or conference that you all experienced, mention it. A lot of people find it funny when someone says what they were thinking too.

Funny Observation

There is a lot of power in seeing the funny side in situations, especially when your observation is both a common reality to the audience but also something that has not often been commented on. This kind of humor will connect the audience to you because you recognize what they're going through in life and they'll appreciate your humor.

Example: The most important skill

"I've got degrees in law and education. I've worked in Europe, Asia and America with people from all over the world. But by far the most important skill I've ever learned is how to fix a photocopier!"

Be Emotional

Strong emotions can be very funny, especially if they involve overreacting. Anger is great because it can be very funny to see someone suffer when they are no threat to you.

Example: The thing that drives me MAD!

It will be funny if I jump up and down on stage shouting:

"Aaaargh! Nothing makes me madder than when I'm trying to get my kids to school on time and I get stuck behind a school bus! And then when it finally moves off, it goes just one house along and stops to pick up the next kid! Aaaargh!"

Double Meaning

Humor is creative and one of the main ways to be creative is to connect two objects or ideas that are seemingly unconnected. You can use this intentionally or spontaneously. If you say something that just comes out in a way that could mean something else, you can draw attention to the different meaning and laugh as you clarify your meaning.

Example: Bear vs. bare

I used an intentional double meaning when telling the story of how I was nearly killed by a grizzly bear in Yellowstone National Park:

"How did I survive? ... Barely!"

Surprise

A lot of humor is based on surprise. As mentioned above, a speaker has an advantage if the audience is not expecting humor. In fact, the more serious an occasion, the easier it is to surprise the audience by saying something funny. The rule of three (see below) is a good device to use surprise humor. It works by saying three different words or three different sentences. The idea is that the audience is expecting all three to be connected and to complement each other. The first two are serious answers and then the third is a humorous surprise.

Example: Surviving countless obstacles

"Throughout all of history, your ancestors survived countless obstacles - war, disease, the British Empire!"

This was to a predominantly American audience. This humor also worked as self-deprecating humor because it was making fun of the fact I am British (when hardly any of the audience was).

Unintentional Humor

Sometimes you might say something that gets an unexpected laugh. That's great! Any laugh is a good laugh. The benefits to the audience are the same. The only thing you must do is make light of it (rather than be embarrassed by it). This is because the audience needs permission to laugh, or rather they won't laugh if they think you don't want them to which then becomes really awkward. Laugh along with them and enjoy the moment.

When the Audience Laughs ...

A final note on laughter is that you should allow the audience to finish laughing. Don't try to continue a speech while they are still laughing as they may not hear you. It also kills the moment and suggests that you don't have a sense of humor. If you can say something else funny to build on the moment and get them laughing again, even better.

5.7 Emotion

There is a reason why listening to someone read a speech can be a very boring experience. Many people read in an emotionless, expressionless manner and are just going through the motions. By contrast, a conversation is rarely boring. When we speak to each other, we tend to speak with passion and also react emotionally. Those are good reasons both to make speeches more conversational and to purposefully include emotion in them. Here are some more reasons to use emotions in your speech.

Emotions Beat Logic

Aristotle taught that the art of persuasion involved three components - logos (appeals to logic and reason), pathos (appeals to emotion and sympathy), and ethos (appeals to the credibility of the speaker). While it is useful to incorporate all of these into a persuasive speech, most people identify more with appeals to emotion. Evidence of this is everywhere in our culture today. News stories are often presented from a human-interest perspective, even when the actual news may be a national or global issue. Put another way, if you were speaking about global warming, your average listener is more likely to be interested in the story of a family losing their home to river flooding than in studying a chart of global carbon dioxide emissions.

Remember that your goal is to connect with your audience so you should consider how your audience might differ from a general audience. If you're speaking to a room full of scientists, they may be more interested in data than various other audiences, although not necessarily. I once attended a keynote speech given to thousands of math teachers. The clear highlight was a funny story about a customer speaking to a call center about his utility bill and the person from call center failing to understand basic math.

Show the Audience You Care

You cannot be passive when you are speaking. You have to show the audience you care because if you don't, why will they? This is why reading a speech well is difficult because a reader has to put a lot of effort in to read it well and make it interesting. The easiest way to show the audience you care is by using your emotions when speaking. In particular, passion and enthusiasm are vital.

Have Fun

One of the biggest lessons I ever learned about speaking is that it is much easier if you are having fun while you do it. The audience will appreciate a sense of playfulness from you as a speaker and likely respond in a similar way. I would argue that you cannot have too much fun in a speech.

Tap Into Their Memories

This is a very powerful tool that every speaker can use to make a stronger connection with their audience. When you paint a scene in your audience's minds, they will fill it with their own images and memories. Sometimes, you can explicitly invite them to remember something from their past.

> **Example: Invite the audience to remember**
>
> Look at the difference between these two story openings:
>
> "I stood outside school on a sunny June afternoon. I was so excited. Term was over. Three months of summer break were just beginning..."
>
> "Think back to your last day of school in the summer. Remember that excitement as you walk out of the building into the sunlight? Three months of summer break stretch ahead of you. I remember that exact feeling when I was 15..."
>
> The second opening is more powerful because it asks the audience to tap into their memories before continuing with the speaker's story.

When the audience members tap into their own memories, the chances are that they will feel happy, the story will become more vivid to them, and therefore they are more likely to remember it.

Negative Emotions

Be careful with more negative emotions (sadness, anger, disgust). I've seen speeches where the speaker has bravely shared stories of terrible traumas that they have suffered. They were so powerful in these moments that it felt as though the audience couldn't recover and get back to a happier place. If the audience relives these traumas with you, it is unfair to leave them at the depths of despair and it will make your job much harder as you continue your speech. Remember that hope and happiness beat depression and sadness and try to balance your speech out so that it has ups as well as downs.

Audiences Remember How You Made Them Feel

Putting all of this section together, audiences will remember how you made them feel, not what you said.* We know that humans have mirror neurons in their brains that can cause them to copy the behaviors of others (e.g., yawning, laughing). As the speaker, you have the perfect opportunity to influence what the audience members are feeling, so you should match the emotion you want your audience to feel. Audiences probably won't remember how they feel if your speech is forgettable and you seem bored so make sure your speech is impactful and engaging.

5.8 Rule of Three

This last technique for connecting with your audience is not going to revolutionize your speech as much as the other techniques in this chapter, but it is very easy to implement which makes it worth knowing about.

The number three is a magical number in speaking. Just as a triangle is the strongest shape, three is the strongest number in speaking and we can use it time and time again. When we hear things in threes they are both pleasing to the ear and easy to remember. Naturally, there may be times when you need to make two or four points, but if you have a genuine choice, three is often the right way to go. We already discussed the rule of three in surprise humor. Here are some other ways to use it.

Structure

When you are structuring a speech, making three points is a good way to go because it is easy for both you and your audience to remember. The attraction of three here is that you are developing your argument better than using just one or two points. However, the bigger danger is when speakers use four or more points. Often the speech becomes a shopping list of points and the audience struggles to remember them or understand which are most important. If you have ten great points, you have two

---

* The earliest derivation of this quote is from Carl W. Buehner: "They may forget what you said – but they will never forget how you made them feel." It is often misattributed to Maya Angelou.

choices. Either select the top three for the audience. Given that we know they will forget most of what they hear, you want to make sure they remember the most important points. Your other choice is to try to group your ten points into three themes so that those themes can perhaps be your three main points and your original ten points are now supporting your themes.

Rhetoric – the Triad

When using the rule of three in parts of speech, the three parts are known as a triad. They can be used as words or phrases. Here are some examples:

"Veni, vidi, vici." ("I came, I saw, I conquered.") - Julius Caesar

"Life, Liberty and the Pursuit of Happiness" - US Declaration of Independence

The Good, the Bad and the Ugly - movie

"Great minds discuss ideas; average minds discuss events; small minds discuss people." – various people

You can see that these can work as a sentence in a speech, or even a structure or speech title.

Physical Space

Photographers often use a rule of thirds for composing their photos. You can use your physical space on stage in the same way. You have a left, center, and right stage to use. You can think about how to use the space for aspects of your speech and stories as well as splitting the audience into thirds the same way and making sure you give each section equal attention.

CHAPTER 6
ONLINE SPEAKING

In this chapter...
6.1 Setup
6.2 Delivery
6.3 Is Online Better or Worse?

As the world shut down in 2020, for many people, working online shifted from being an occasional activity to becoming the main way of meeting, working, doing business, and even going to school. Since then, online speaking has shown its value and will probably remain with us forever. This chapter is not going to recommend specific equipment or software but will focus on the main considerations and adaptations to public speaking when you are online.

6.1 Setup

Sound

Your sound quality is by far the most important aspect of online speaking in much the same way that your voice is the most important delivery skill. If your audience cannot clearly hear you then speaking is pointless. Some of your audience may also choose just to listen to you (as on a podcast) and may not be concerned about your video.

The most important issue to decide is whether or not to get a microphone to connect to your computer or whether to use the computer's inbuilt microphone. If using the inbuilt microphone, test it and check with other people to see if they can hear you clearly. You will also want to identify where the actual microphone is on the computer so that you do not obstruct it or make distracting noises near it.

If you want to get the best sound possible, a microphone will undoubtedly provide better quality sound.

Video

The next most important consideration after sound is your video quality. Ideally, this should be high definition, but check that your computer and internet speed can cope with this and will not lag. There are three key factors to getting great video quality.

- **Camera** – A high-quality webcam will capture good video. If you are using an in-built camera on your computer, you may want to test it to see if it is adequate.
- **Lighting** – Good lighting significantly improves the quality of your video including your camera's ability to capture a detailed image.

Make sure you are lit in front of you rather than behind you. Most important is to light up your face so that your online audience can clearly see you and your expressions. You can buy cheap ring lights to do this if your room does not have enough natural or artificial lighting.

- **Camera position** – Ideally your camera should be in front of you and level with you so that you are not looking up or down into it. If you are using a laptop camera, raise the laptop up (e.g., on a pile of books) so that it is level with you.

Software

Familiarize yourself with whatever software programs you are using to present. You do not want to be in the middle of a presentation trying to work out how to share your screen! You also want the best internet connection possible to reduce the chances of lagging or being cut off while speaking.

Environment

Prepare your environment for online speaking. Ideally, it should be somewhere quiet so that no noise interferes with your presentation. Will you be standing or sitting for your talk? Standing will give you more energy. Sitting may be more relaxed.

Think about your background behind you. If you choose the actual background from your room where you are speaking, is it clean and visually appealing? Are there any distractions? You might prefer an artificial background using green screen technology but be careful that this is not distracting. Moving backgrounds can be distracting as well as the fact that green screen technology sometimes does not capture all of your face or something you wish to show to your audience online.

6.2 Delivery

Presenting Online

- **Eye contact** – One of the trickiest differences with online speaking is knowing where to look. Ideally, when speaking you should look into your webcam because this will then look as if you are directly looking at your audience, which will engage them more and make you look more sincere. If you are looking at your audience (or yourself) on screen then you will not be looking directly into the camera. Sometimes I stick arrows pointing to my webcam to remind me where to look.

- **Energy** – It will naturally be harder for you and your audience to have as much energy as you might have at a live event. As a speaker, standing can give you more energy. Although you are not with your audience, you can directly address any of them individually or collectively through the internet and ask them to respond. Such responses could be physical (talking, thumbs up, waving, hands up) or through the chat. Because online speaking is more static than speaking in-person, try to think of ways to break up your presentation so that the audience does not feel like they are doing the same thing for too long. You can create virtual breaks in your talk by showing the audience a video or using online breakout rooms. Remember to include actual breaks as well.

- **Space** – As a presenter, you have a lot less space to use when you are sitting or standing behind a desk. You will probably not be able to change camera angles. Think about what (if anything) you may need to show the audience and how you can do it in a confined space. Can you use online tools instead of showing something physical?

Online Engagement

When you are not physically in the same room as your audience it is harder to engage them. They may have many distractions around them that you are unable to control. It is therefore really important to try to make online presentations as engaging as possible. Here are some possible ways:

- **Cameras on** – This may seem obvious, but the first battle is to encourage as many of your online viewers as possible to turn their cameras on. This makes it feel more alive and real for all concerned. As well as requesting this directly, there are more subtle ways you can use such as asking for smiles, waves, thumbs up, or even taking a screenshot picture of all attendees. Calling out particular attendees by name also gives them a reason to stay alert with their cameras on.

- **Chat** – The chat feature is a benefit to online speaking provided that attendees use it to engage with you or your presentation and not to spam it with irrelevant messages. Using this feature is using visual engagement (reading) and kinesthetic engagement (typing) but be careful that the audience is still listening to you too. If you are asking them all to respond to something by using the chat, you may want to give them time to do so rather than just continuing to speak. You can offer a commentary on the responses as they come in. I've also seen speakers offer freebies at the very end of a presentation by picking random names from attendees who participated in the chat. This encouraged attendees to be particularly active in the chat to increase their chances of winning.

- **Breakout rooms** – Using breakout rooms can change the dynamics of a presentation by moving attendees into smaller, more intimate groups where they can discuss a relevant topic, in much the same way you can create small groups to discuss issues in a live meeting. Be careful not to send people away for too long though as there are always risks that they have not understood what they are supposed to be doing or that they go off-task. As the online presenter, you can go around the different breakout rooms, but remember that the more there are, the harder it is to be there for everyone.

- **Quizzes** – You can make up your own quizzes by asking questions live and asking for responses in the chat (or on camera) or you can use software apps to do this. Some apps allow participants to use their phones to respond to questions and the answers can be displayed in real-time on the presentation screen.
- **Music and video** – If you are online anyway, it is easy to share music or video clips to illustrate a point and enhance engagement. Make sure you have permission to use anything you are showing. Remember that there can be a slight lag between sound and pictures online and it is also better to embed videos in your presentation than to be streaming them live from the internet.

6.3 Is Online Better or Worse?

You may be in a position where you have a choice between speaking in person, online, or hybrid (where there is a live event and also an online link for people to watch). When comparing them, each has its advantages and disadvantages. The main ones are listed on the following pages for you to consider.

In-person Meetings

Advantages

- This is the traditional format that most people are used to.
- As a speaker, it is much easier to bring energy to a live event.
- You can also connect with your audience more directly (by seeing all of them at once and hearing them laugh).
- There may be more perceived value in presenting in person rather than online.

Disadvantages

- It takes time, money, effort, and usually travel to go to a venue to speak.
- There may be a smaller potential audience as attendees are more likely to have come locally.
- As a speaker, you do not usually have much control of your speaking environment in the way you do at home.

Online Meetings

Advantages

- Online meetings are cheap and easy to organize.
- People can attend from all over the world while still in their own homes. This means you can reach far wider audiences.
- You can easily record the meeting.
- You can make eye contact with everyone at the same time (by looking into the camera).
- You can see the names of attendees and respond to them both in person and in the chat.
- The chat feature is an easy way for attendees to ask questions as you are speaking. You can respond to these in real-time or in the Q&A section.
- You can share documents and internet links online as you speak.

Disadvantages

- It can be harder to bring energy to online meetings, especially if your audience has been overwhelmed with a lot of other online meetings.
- You cannot always see all participants on screen. When participants turn off their cameras, they are more likely to be distracted.
- You are at the mercy of the technology gods! If the technology falters (such as losing your internet connection), you cannot just carry on speaking.
- Security can be harder to manage online if it is easy for strangers to attend and disrupt a meeting.
- You also need to manage attendees who have not muted their computers and may be making noise.

Hybrid Meetings

Advantages

- The best of both worlds where attendees can choose their preference for how they wish to attend.
- Potentially, the highest attendance.
- Switching between acknowledging in-person and online attendees may provide natural breaks in your presentation.

Disadvantages

- If you (the speaker) are the only person running the meeting, it will take extra work to monitor the online attendees while also speaking to your live audience.
- You may have to adjust some live activities that would not work as well for online attendees.
- Will online attendees be able to see and follow everything that is happening live?
- If the camera is fixed, the speaker may have less room to move than normal (without going off camera).
- An extra person may be needed to direct the camera and monitor online participants and chat.

CHAPTER 7
SPECIFIC EVENTS

This book has prepared you to speak in any situation. However, you might find yourself at a specific occasion where there are particular considerations you should give to your speech. These considerations should form part of your inquiries at the context stage (see Chapter 1) where you find out what is required of you. This chapter gives a brief guide to the main considerations for some of the most popular types of specific occasion speech.

7.1 Work Presentations

What's Different?

We have discussed work presentations a lot throughout this book but here are some key points to remember. Your audience is probably professional and may include colleagues or clients. The presentation is likely to be focused on a particular, clear objective or outcome such as informing, persuading or selling. You may have a lot of raw information and data from which to create your speech and you may be expected to use slides. Everyone's time is very important so you should make sure everything you present is relevant.

What to do

- It is essential that you understand the context of your presentation (see Chapter 1) so that you present what is required and stay very focused.
- Make sure you understand the information you are presenting. Use your experience, knowledge and research to master the content you present. Use your Speech Map (see Chapter 3) to be clear about the overall message and structure of your speech (i.e. where you are going and how you are getting there).
- You can still use advanced techniques such as stories and humor to connect with your audience but make sure they are not wasting time or a substitute for the essential content you need to present.
- Make sure you start and finish on time and are respectful of everyone's time.
- Be prepared to adjust your presentation if you can tell your audience wants more or less of something you are covering.
- If you need to use slides to assist your presentation, make sure they are useful and relevant. More information about the effective use of slides is covered in Chapter 3.4 (Speech Materials) and Chapter 4 (Technology Practice).

- Anticipate potential questions and prepare in advance any answers that you can. More advice about questions and answers is in Chapter 4.3 (Delivery).
- Have a clear call to action or next steps if appropriate. Be prepared to follow up with additional information or answers to questions after the presentation.
- Be appropriately professional but you can still be friendly!

What not to do

- Do not waste time or repeat what everyone already knows. If some people in your audience know less than others, bring them up to speed as simply and quickly as you can.
- Do not overcomplicate what you are presenting or overuse jargon. Remember that simplicity is the key and will be appreciated. This is especially true of facts, statistics and data. If there is a lot of information that the audience needs, then you can always let them take that away (or send it to them in advance). Your role in presenting should be to highlight the key points.
- Do not apologize for being there or make excuses about feeling unprepared. Act appropriately confident even if you do not feel it (see Chapter 2 – Fake it Till You Make it).

7.2 Introductions and Thank-you Speeches

What's Different?

You may find yourself called upon to introduce or thank a speaker at an event. The request may be well in advance or it might be relatively last minute (such as when an organizer asks you to introduce the speaker moments before they go on stage or thank them just before they come off stage). If a speaker gives you an introduction to read, you are not in control of the words, but you must do your best to deliver them well.

What to do

- If possible, contact the person you are introducing to get their written introduction or find out how they would like to be introduced.
- If you are given a written introduction, read it and practice reading it. Familiarize yourself with any words or names that are tricky to pronounce.
- If you are using your own introduction of a speaker, use a simple structure such as:
    - Enthusiastic explanation of who you are introducing.
    - Brief anecdote or story of when you met them, or something that happened together, or something that the person has done.
    - Brief introduction to why they are there and/or what they are speaking about.
    - Ask the audience to welcome them as they come on stage.
- For thank-you speeches, make sure you have listened to what they spoke about.
- Follow a simple structure such as:
    - Thank the speaker for their presentation.

- Refer to one thing you learned from it or how you might apply what you learned to your life.
- Ask the audience to join you in thanking them again.

What not to do

- Do not paraphrase what a speaker has written in their introduction. Read it as they wrote it.
- Do not try to steal the limelight from the speaker.
- Don't look bored or unenthusiastic!

7.3 Weddings

What's Different?

Weddings are very happy occasions. Depending on your relationship to the couple, there are likely to be lots of people you know and lots you don't know. By the time you are speaking, people are likely to have started drinking which means they may be more relaxed, but potentially also rowdy!

What to do

- Regardless of who you are, your speech is probably going to honor the married couple, thank the people who organized the wedding, thank everyone for coming and finish with a toast to the newlyweds.
- Focus on stories that show your connection to either or both of the married couple, funny things they've done, and anything that shows their love for each other.
- Humor is great but make sure it can be laughed off and will not genuinely embarrass the person you are talking about.
- If you are one of the newlyweds:
    - Thank everyone who came, the parents and people in the wedding party for organizing the wedding.
    - Focus on your love for your spouse. You will never have a better time to be sentimental. Tell a story about how you met or how you grew together and what they mean to you.
    - Express your hopes for the future.
- If you are a parent of one of the newlyweds:
    - You will have a lot of sentimentality and emotion on your side. You can tap into this by relating an early memory from their childhood.
    - You can talk about your first impressions when you met their partner and how you've seen their relationship develop.

- You should wish the married couple well for the future and toast them.
- If you are the best man or maid of honor:
  - It is probably your job to say something funny about the groom (if you are the best man) or the bride (if you are the maid of honor). The best humor will not be totally shocking but will relate experiences or qualities about them, which will make sense to the audience when considering who you are talking about.
  - You will want to say something nice about the bride (if you are the best man) or the groom (if you are the maid of honor) which could include first impressions when you met them or how they changed their spouse's life.
  - You should wish the bride and groom well for the future and toast them.

What not to do

- Don't ruin the day! Don't offend anyone, especially not the bride, or the families of the married couple. If you are thinking of saying things that you are not sure of, it probably makes sense not to say them.
- Don't talk about previous boyfriends, girlfriends, or marriages!
- Don't speak for too long. At this point, everyone is anticipating food or dancing so a short, sweet, funny speech is better than a long, boring one.

7.4 Funerals

What's Different?

Eulogies at funerals are difficult because everyone is mourning and there is considerable emotion involved.

What to do

- The most important thing is to honor the life of the deceased person. Think about the stories and anecdotes from that person's life as well as your personal connection to the deceased.
- You may find that using a simple speech structure or theme is helpful for creating and delivering your speech. For example, if you use three main points, they could each be a quality the deceased possessed or they could be three different stories, events, or stages from that person's life.
- (Respectful) humor is often very much appreciated. Though funerals are sad, people want to have happy memories of the deceased. Telling anything funny that they once did is likely to bring smiles and laughs.
- Carry a written copy of your speech in case emotion takes over and you need help remembering it. In a worst-case scenario, you can even give it to someone else to read.
- Carry tissues just in case.

What not to do

- Don't offend anyone present. If the eulogy is part of a religious service, make sure it is appropriate to that setting.

7.5 Acceptance Speeches

What's Different?

Accepting an award is an unusual type of speech because the focus is on you but if you just make a speech about yourself or thank everyone you know, it will be boring.

What to do

- Understand how much time you have. A shorter speech is likely to be appreciated more than a longer one.
- Thank the person or organization giving you the award (or that chose you for it) and explain how much it means to you.
- If you won the award ahead of other people, acknowledge and honor them.
- Thank others that personally helped you to the extent necessary but keep this list to a minimum, especially if the audience does not personally know who you are talking about. If there are lots of people who contributed to your success, find a way to thank them personally outside the speech where you have more time and can do so more personally (e.g., a written tribute).
- Do you have a key story or lesson from (a) your experience that led to the award, or (b) your life generally that will entertain and inform the audience? Often the audience may only know you in the capacity for which you won the award, so if you can share something more personal with them it will connect them to you.

What not to do

- Do not go overtime!
- Do not be arrogant, boastful, or ungrateful.
- Don't feign surprise at winning (but of course show it if it is genuine).

7.6 Impromptu Speaking

What's Different?

If public speaking is scary generally, impromptu speaking is most people's nightmare. This is where you are called upon to speak in a situation with little or no time to prepare.

What to do

- Stay calm! Breathe! Take a moment to compose yourself.
- Use whatever time you have available to prepare your answer or speech. For example, if you have five minutes, use it to structure your speech quickly. If you are asked to come on stage to say something, use the walk up there to start composing a response.
- If you are answering a question, you might want to repeat the question to make sure you have heard and understood it correctly. This also buys you a little time to start composing your answer.
- It is fine to take a few seconds to think about what you are going to say. After that, you need to start speaking.
- If you can think of something funny to say at the outset, you can instantly connect with your audience.
- Try to outline a simple Speech Map (or structure) for your speech. For example:
  - Introduction
  - 3 points / funny story / problem and solution / past and present analysis
  - Conclusion
- When you start speaking, if you are answering a question, your answer will either have come to you and you now have a complete outline of your Speech Map or you won't yet know where you are going as you set off. If you don't know where you are going with your answer, explore a few possibilities before perhaps concluding with what you think is the best answer. If you genuinely don't know

what to say to answer a question then say so while offering an answer that may still have value or insight in a connected area.

- Try to take control of your speech by having fun and showing passion. Don't make it look like you are being tortured.
- Practice whenever you can. I often mentally answer questions in situations where someone is speaking and I'm thinking, "What would I say if I had to answer that question?" Toastmasters meetings have a section of the meeting devoted to Table Topics (impromptu speaking). The more you do it the easier it becomes.

What not to do

- Don't panic! Don't stop breathing! Don't rush into speaking without composing yourself.
- Don't complain about being asked to speak at the last minute but you might be able to joke about it.
- Don't ramble on with no end in sight hoping that someone else takes control of your speech. Only you can control it!
- Don't get upset when you have finished. It is very common to think of something you could have said when you sit back down. Save it for next time.

7.7 Job Interviews

What's Different?

There is a lot at stake in a job interview because you are using your speaking to try to get a job. Unlike most other public speaking situations, you are not fully in control but are responding to your interviewer and you may have to follow up your answers a number of times as the interviewer reacts.

What to do

- Make sure you have done your research on the job, company, and people interviewing you. Try and work some of this into your answers or questions.
- Be authentic. You want the interviewer to get to see who you really are and what you can do. They will need to see this to know if you will be a good fit for the job.
- Be interested. A bored or rude candidate will never get the job.
- Be friendly because they might be your future boss or colleague.
- Be confident in your abilities (but you can explain away any nerves by saying how much the job means to you).
- Have a plan of points/skills/experience you want to make to the interviewer and use your answers to fit them in. Do this appropriately though so you are definitely answering the question and not evading it!
- Listen carefully to what the interviewer says and try to respond or incorporate some of what they say into your answers or questions, so they can tell you've taken it on board.
- Plan answers to all the "classic interview questions" such as:
    - Why did you leave your last job?
    - Why do you want this job?
    - What is your greatest weakness?
    - Describe a time when you had to overcome an obstacle. How did you overcome it?
    - What's the hardest thing you've ever done?

- Describe a problem/conflict at work. How did you resolve it?
- How do you handle pressure/stress?

What not to do

- Avoid showing weakness. If asked a question such as, "What is your greatest weakness?" have an answer prepared about something specific you are working on to improve or gain more experience, but make sure it is not a skill that is essential for the job.
- Don't exaggerate your achievements. You can explain your accomplishments in the best possible light but you want them to be true.
- Avoid using jargon words or job descriptions to describe your past experience as these can be confusing or the interviewer may assume you're trying to make your past experience sound more impressive than it really is. Instead communicate as clearly as possible.

7.8 Local Meetings

What's Different?

You may be active in your community and find yourself speaking before a local committee or school committee. Usually, this will be in public in front of a number of committee members or officials.

What to do

- Understand the issue you are speaking about and do your research.
- Get to the point. Meetings like this are usually long with many people speaking and attention can wane. Make sure you stay within the time allotted to speak.
- Remember to include the human impact of your issue. Stories of locally affected people not only affect people's emotions but are also relevant.
- Don't be afraid to be emotional to show how much you care or are affected by an issue.
- Present new information. Nothing is more tedious than hearing the same point repeated endlessly.
- Try to be constructive and positive where possible (including presenting solutions if possible). It will help your argument if you appear to be on the side of the committee you are addressing rather than against them.

What not to do

- Don't let your emotions overcome you so much that you cannot make the points you wish to.
- Don't be angry (unless you really think a situation merits it). Usually, anger will not help the people you are addressing solve an issue, nor will it scare them into adopting your idea.
- Don't be a serial complainer. Even if your complaints are valid, people will eventually stop listening to you!

7.9 Panel Discussions

What's Different?

When you speak on a panel, you are not alone. You and a number of other speakers will be speaking and answering questions from a moderator and audience.

What to do

- Listen carefully to what the other panelists say including, questions asked and previous answers given.
- When you know the topic the panel is speaking about, have a plan of points you want to make and anticipate questions where you can fit them in.
- Do not simply repeat answers already given. Either agree with them and explain why, build upon their answers, or explain why you think differently.
- Be respectful to the other panelists and do not interrupt them. If you disagree, do so respectfully.
- If you are a moderator on a panel, balance the need to give all the panelists a chance to speak along with picking the best person to answer specific questions. Prepare questions to ask the panelists if the audience is reluctant to ask any.

What not to do

- Do not try to dominate the event if you are one of many panelists.

7.10 Pitches

What's Different?

A pitch is a specific type of persuasive speech where you are seeking investment or selling an idea or product. If you are pitching a business opportunity or investment, your audience (e.g., investors) may be different from the product or service's target audience.

What to do

- Be very clear about the product or service you demonstrating:
    - What does it do?
    - How does it work?
    - What is unique or special about it?
    - Why is it needed?
    - What problem does it solve?
- Be very clear who your pitch audience is and pitch to them. Why should your audience care about it? What is your value proposition to them?
- Be very clear what you are asking for. If you are asking for investment:
    - How will the investor get their money back?
    - How have you valued your service or business?
    - What will you do with the investment?
- Why are you the person pitching? What is your story behind the product or service?
- Show your passion for what you are pitching because if you are not enthusiastic about it, why would anyone else be?
- Be realistic. When people invest in you they want to know that you are not just dreaming.
- Be prepared for questions you might be asked. Ideally, try to answer them in your pitch.

What not to do

- Don't presume your ideas and knowledge are easily understood by others. You may have worked on something for a long time and it makes sense to you but you should consider whether others will understand it or if you need to simplify your explanations.

7.11 Kids' and School Presentations

What's Different?

You might be a child reading this or a teacher who is responsible for getting children to present in class or at a school event. The stakes are high here. Many adults list a terrible experience speaking in public at school as the reason why they've had a lifelong fear of public speaking. An audience of school children may not be as understanding as a normal audience so teachers should do their utmost to create a safe, respectful, and supportive environment for the speakers. Feedback to the children should also be overwhelmingly positive and constructive.

What to do

- Speak so that you can be heard! This is the biggest mistake made by children (and allowed by teachers). Raise your voice, speak into the microphone (if there is one), and speak clearly.
- Practice your speech, even if it is just by yourself at home.
- Try to speak without notes. If you have to read your speech, make sure you have practiced it so you are fluent and can read with appropriate expression and pauses.
- Face your audience and look at them. Find friendly faces (e.g., the teacher, friends) and avoid distracting or silly faces.
- Stand up straight and keep your hands out of your pockets.
- Remember to breathe!
- Try to enjoy the experience. If you speak well, many adults will be impressed as it's a skill they find difficult.

What not to do

- Don't rush through speaking. This includes not starting before you have the audience's attention, not speaking too quickly, and not starting to walk off before you've finished speaking.

- Don't hide your face behind paper or by turning around to look at a whiteboard or display.
- If you are part of a group, make sure you do not block the speaker and are not doing anything distracting while they speak.
- Do not panic if something goes wrong. It's not the end of the world!

7.12 Competition Debating

What's Different?

There are many different formats for debating which have very specific and different rules. The following is general advice only.

Debating is different because:

- You are usually doing it in teams.
- You are arguing against the other side.
- You get to respond to the other side.
- You may not get to choose the side you are arguing, so you may not personally believe in what you have to argue.

What to do

- Know the rules and requirements of the debate format.
- Remember a debate is an intellectual argument. Make the best arguments you can even if you don't personally believe them.
- Make sure you introduce yourself clearly and make it clear which side you are arguing for.
- Have a clear structure to your speech so the audience and judges can follow your arguments.
- Be firm but respectful to your opponents.
- Work with your team so that you complement each other and build on each other's arguments or add new arguments.
- Listen very carefully to the other side's arguments so that you can rebut them.
- Adapt to arguments made so that you are thinking and responding in real-time, not just saying what you were going to say anyway.
- As well as factual research, think about stories and experiences you can bring to the arguments.
- Have a clear closing sentence summarizing your arguments.

What not to do

- Do not simply repeat what your teammates said.
- Do not insult the other speakers.
- Do not be distracting while others are speaking.
- Do not use superlative (or exaggerated) language unless you can justify it. For example, if you say "We should abolish homework because *every* kid on earth hates homework," the other side only has to find one kid that doesn't hate it to disprove the claim.

7.13 Toastmasters Contests

What's Different?

Toastmasters International is an organization where you can join a local club and practice public speaking. Every year it organizes different types of speech competition which start at the local club level and go up to the wider district level (evaluation contest, humor contest, Table Topics® contest, tall tales contest) or to the World Championship of Public Speaking (international speech contest).

What to do

- Carefully read the latest speech contest rulebook for your particular competition. Make sure you understand the rules and requirements and follow them.
- Read the judging criteria so you understand what the judges are looking for in the contest.
- Speak to others who have competed before or study their speeches online.
- In the international speech contest:
  - Choose an important topic that will appeal to the greatest number of people with a message to benefit them.
  - Use stories and dialogue to illustrate your points.
  - Be memorable and original.
- In the evaluation speech contest:
  - Create a structure for your speech, not just a list of points.
  - Be positive and enthusiastic about what the speaker you are evaluating did well.
  - Offer constructive tips about the most important areas for improvement and demonstrate how they might be applied.
- In the Table Topics® (impromptu speaking) contest:
  - Take a moment to reflect on your answer before you start speaking.

- Try (quickly) to create a structure for your speech (such as – opening, story illustrating your connection to the question, answering the question with another story, closing).
- Make sure you try to answer the question specifically rather than offer obviously preprepared anecdotes.
- If you are not sure how to answer the question, start by exploring potential answers in the first half of your speech before deciding on an actual answer in the second half of your speech.
- If you have no idea how to answer a question then make a connection to the next closest thing and give an answer about that.

- Use humor in your speech.
- Practice your actual speech (or the type of speech if it is an evaluation or Table Topics®).
- Compete for the right reasons. The right reasons are not to win, but to learn and grow as a speaker (and to enjoy the experience)! Be gracious, whatever the result.

What not to do

- Do not go undertime or overtime as you will be disqualified.
- Do not copy others' stories or speeches and present them as your own.
- Do not lie or make up stories that you are presenting as true.

7.14 TED Talks

What's Different?

TED and TEDx talks are all about "Ideas Worth Spreading." To get accepted you will need to apply to a specific event with your speech idea.

What to do

- Look at the TED rules and guidelines on the ted.com website.
- You should have an "Idea Worth Spreading" which forms the focus of your talk. This can be a new, surprising idea or an existing idea with a new argument behind it that changes perspective on it. The talk should make it clear how the audience can benefit from this new idea.
- Make sure it is clear why you are the person giving your talk. What is your experience or background that makes you the perfect person to give it?
- Focus on the human connection in your talk. Storytelling is an essential ingredient of a good talk.
- Make sure your talk is 18 minutes or less.
- Be conversational.
- Stay in the red dot on stage.

What not to do

- Do not talk about any taboo subjects. For TED, these are:
  - Commercials or sales talks for something you are selling.
  - Politics.
  - Religion (if you are trying to convert people or prove the correctness of a particular religion or similar belief).
  - Pseudoscience (as there must be a proper scientific basis underpinning any scientific claims).
- Do not use slides unless they add something valuable to your speech.

Acknowledgments

I never intended to write a book about speaking! Though I've loved speaking all my life, I didn't think the world needed another. But after repeatedly witnessing speakers of all experience levels struggle with creating and delivering speeches, I wanted to help everyone by showing how simple the process should be.

Every time I listen to someone speak, I'm learning something, so I'd like to acknowledge every person who I've had the pleasure of listening to (or coaching) over the years, as well as all those people who have listened to me and given me feedback, and of course everyone I've competed against in a speech contest. Listed below are just some of you but all of you have helped me on my speaking journey (and life) and I can't thank you enough.

My family of speakers:
Kat, Jonathan, Jasmine, Mike, Sue, Ray and Zara. All of you are such talented speakers!

Speech Coaches:
My wonderful network of speech coaches including Rick Pollak, Craig Millar, Claudio Sennhauser, Nathan Gold, Scottie Spurzem, Massimo Peroncelli, Susan Trumpler, and Michael Marchuk.

National Speakers Association:
Linda Stacy, Roger Grannis, Pam Garramone, Matt Ward, Tamsen Webster, Theresa Rose, Julie Brown, Jana Scholten, Dan Junkins, and all the members of NSA New England.

Toastmasters:
Ed Skurka, Wayne Braverman, Tom Nyzio, Esther Paris, Lynn and Chuck Potter, Angela Nuss, Sean DaSilva, Rick Winer, Stefano McGee, Sherri Raftery, Merrill Winoker, Wenjie Cheng, Kristen Chin, Stacey Shipman,

Lyson Ludvic, Joe Grondin, Andrew Kneebone, Palaniappa Subramaniam, Jeff Davis, Kingi Biddle, Olivia Schofield, Brian Woolf, Sarah Khan, Dave Cohen, Christabel Bensam, Keith Fredericks, everyone at Providence Toastmasters Club and Foxboro Achievers Toastmasters Club, all the Toastmasters of District 31 (Massachusetts and Rhode Island), and all those I have met around the world.

A special thanks to the World Champions who I have learned so much from and who inspire me: Darren LaCroix, Ed Tate, Mark Brown, Lance Miller, Craig Valentine, Jim Key, Ryan Avery, Pres Vasilev, Dananjaya Hettiarrachchi, Manoj Vasudevan, and Aaron Beverly.

Improv:
Lizzie Roderick and Lauren Powers (two amazing instructors) and all the people I performed sketches with.

Students:
John Zhu who has provided a steady stream of students for me to coach and all of the kids I've had the fun of coaching.

Teachers:
Mrs. Quintrell, Alastair Endersby, Richard Moxham and Ed Peel – thank you for each giving me my early speaking opportunities!
Brian Joyce – thank you for all your encouragement and support!

About the Author

If you've just read this book then you already know a lot about me because I've shared many of my speaking experiences. Some of my speaking highlights are coming 3rd in the Toastmasters World Championship of Public Speaking and winning the District 31 International Speech Contest six times. My coaching highlights include helping TEDx speakers, professional speakers, corporate presenters, founders' pitches and contest winners.

If you are interested in keynote speeches, workshops or individual coaching, visit: **www.lastminutespeaking.com** or **www.stuartpink.com**.

Stuart Pink
Speech Coach, Professional Speaker at Last
Minute Speaking

Also published:
Brainarium – Exercise Your Creativity
Read this book to learn how to be creative in any situation!

Made in the USA
Middletown, DE
24 June 2023

33332533R00146